YORK NOTES

The Mill on the Floss

George Eliot

Notes by Kathryn Simpson

 Longman   York Press

The right of Kathryn Simpson to be identified as Author of this Work has been asserted by him in accordance with the Copyright, Designs and Patents Act 1988

YORK PRESS
322 Old Brompton Road, London SW5 9JH

PEARSON EDUCATION LIMITED
Edinburgh Gate, Harlow,
Essex CM20 2JE, United Kingdom
Associated companies, branches and representatives throughout the world

First published 1999
Fifth impression 2003

ISBN 0-582-41472-5

Designed by Vicki Pacey, Trojan Horse, London
Phototypeset by Gem Graphics, Trenance, Mawgan Porth, Cornwall
Colour reproduction and film output by Spectrum Colour
Produced by Pearson Education Asia Limited, Hong Kong

CONTENTS

PART ONE

INTRODUCTION

HOW TO STUDY A NOVEL

Studying a novel on your own requires self-discipline and a carefully thought-out work plan in order to be effective.

- You will need to read the novel more than once. Start by reading it quickly for pleasure, then read it slowly and thoroughly.
- On your second reading make detailed notes on the plot, characters and themes of the novel. Further readings will generate new ideas and help you to memorise the details of the story.
- Some of the characters will develop as the plot unfolds. How do your responses towards them change during the course of the novel?
- Think about how the novel is narrated. From whose point of view are events described?
- A novel may or may not present events chronologically: the time-scheme may be a key to its structure and organisation.
- What part do the settings play in the novel?
- Are words, images or incidents repeated so as to give the work a pattern? Do such patterns help you to understand the novel's themes?
- Identify what styles of language are used in the novel.
- What is the effect of the novel's ending? Is the action completed and closed, or left incomplete and open?
- Does the novel present a moral and just world?
- Cite exact sources for all quotations, whether from the text itself or from critical commentaries. Wherever possible find your own examples from the novel to back up your opinions.
- Always express your ideas in your own words.

This York Note offers an introduction to *The Mill on the Floss* and cannot substitute for close reading of the text and the study of secondary sources.

The Mill on the Floss is an absorbing tragedy of ordinary lives, of family discord and financial ruin, of sibling love and bitterness, of intense illicit desires, betrayal, and moral conflict. Although this plot may seem to verge on the melodramatic, George Eliot maintains throughout a finely balanced tension between passion and morality, sadness and comedy, desire and duty, and individual and social needs. The novel stirs an emotional response which is balanced by its engagement with many of the controversial intellectual issues of the day: about God and belief, origins and destiny, industrial progress and the future of society, and about the position of women and male–female relations.

One biographer called George Eliot 'the voice of the century', and indeed she was. This is not because she articulated what we may now see as the 'solidity' and stuffy moralism of the Victorian Age, however, but because she expressed its immense uncertainties. It was a period of great social and cultural upheaval and George Eliot in many ways epitomised this, as one sketch of her life suggests:

> Marian Evans (George Eliot) could be considered one of the century's most famous real-life *femmes fatales*: intellectually rapacious, she renounced religion, assumed a man's name (professionally), lived with another woman's husband, and on his death married a man twenty years her junior. She was admired and feared, celebrated and socially shunned, iconoclastic and wedded to intellectual integrity.
>
> (Kimberley Reynolds and Nicola Humble, *Victorian Heroines: Representations of Femininity in Nineteenth-Century Literature and Art*, Harvester Wheatsheaf, 1993, pp. 89–90)

The Mill on the Floss is George Eliot's most autobiographical novel and deals in part with her personal pain at the loss of the close sibling bonds with her beloved brother Isaac, who had cut off all contact with her, and with her sister Chrissey, who had died whilst George Eliot was still writing her novel. It also marked a turning point in George Eliot's career, since her real identity as a scandalous woman and free-thinking intellectual had become known. When first published, the novel provoked a storm of objections from critics who felt that their morals had been compromised in being drawn into the sordid lives of George Eliot's characters. However, it makes a strong case for the need for tolerance and understanding of difference which George Eliot saw as vital in a period of great social transition. The technique of **omniscient narration** is one conventionally employed in nineteenth-century novels, but here it has the specific purpose of eliciting the readers' sympathy and tolerance. We are drawn into the world of this novel as participants, as is immediately apparent in the opening pages. The narrator shares his dream with us and we are invited to hear the story of the Tullivers at his fireside.

The Mill on the Floss remains a provocative novel and critics still debate the troubling issues it raises. This is partly because it refuses to reduce complex moral issues about belief, behaviour, sexuality or sexual politics to a simple formula. We are offered no easy solutions to the moral complexities it raises, but instead we are invited to use our intellect and emotion, insight and feeling, to reach our own interpretation.

PART TWO

SUMMARIES & COMMENTARIES

The Mill on the Floss was first published in April 1860 in three volumes. The second edition was published in two volumes later that year, and the third in one volume in December 1862. It was published again in two volumes for the Cabinet edition of *The Works of George Eliot* in 1878; this was at the time of George Henry Lewes's final illness and George Eliot did see not the proofs for this edition. George Eliot did not correct proofs for the second edition, although for the third she corrected a copy of the second edition of the novel. It is this third edition which was used for the Cabinet edition and which is usually taken as the text in new editions of the novel.

The text used in compiling these Notes is the Penguin Classics edition (1985).

SYNOPSIS

After describing his dream, the narrator resumes his story of the lives of the Tulliver family thirty years previously. At the centre of this story is the problematic relationship between the two Tulliver children, Tom and Maggie, and the plot revolves around the demise of this family's fortunes. The Tullivers live at Dorlcote Mill, near to the provincial trading town of St Ogg's, and in the first chapters we are given a sense of their lifestyle and the relationships between them. Mr Tulliver, a respectable and apparently successful miller, has decided to give Tom a good education, although it is the more intelligent Maggie (her father's favourite) who would clearly be more suited to this. On the advice of his friend, Mr Riley, Mr Tulliver will send Tom to be educated by Reverend Stelling. In the first book of the novel, the great divisions between the Tullivers and Mrs Tulliver's family, the Dodsons, are made evident as is the dire financial situation in which Mr Tulliver is soon to find himself as a result of his various loans and rash involvement in lawsuits over water rights.

Before Tom goes to Mr Stelling he is to spend his spring holiday at home and Maggie eagerly awaits his return. The idyllic reunion she hopes for is made impossible when Tom discovers that through Maggie's neglect his rabbits have died. Maggie's tendency to be forgetful is the source of many of her childhood difficulties, and lapses of responsibility have damaging consequences in her adult life too. Her attachment to Tom is very strong and her emotional nature leads her to extremes of behaviour (pushing her angelic cousin Lucy into the mud in a fit of jealousy, running away to the gypsies, and later, cutting off her hair). By contrast, Tom is controlled, authoritarian and self-righteous. He withdraws his love as punishment for Maggie's neglect, and she goes, as usual, to the attic. By the evening their friendship is mended and the following day they go fishing together.

At Mr Stelling's, Tom struggles with his studies. Maggie's first visit demonstrates her intelligence and eagerness to learn what Tom is failing to grasp. Returning to the Stellings' after his Christmas holidays, he finds that his new fellow-pupil is Philip Wakem, the son of his father's arch enemy. An uneasy friendship develops between them, though this is improved temporarily by Maggie's second visit. Maggie and Philip form a close bond and promise always to be friends. Maggie goes to school with Lucy.

When Maggie is thirteen, she is summoned home by her father, who has lost his lawsuit and is now bankrupt. By the time Maggie arrives home he has collapsed following his discovery that Mr Wakem has bought the mortgage on the Mill. Maggie immediately goes to Mr Stelling's to tell Tom and to bring him home. The aunts and uncles refuse to help the Tullivers financially and all of their possessions are sold to pay off some of their debts. The meanness of the Dodson sisters and their husbands contrasts with the generosity of Bob Jakin, Tom's childhood friend. At this early stage there is some hope that Guest and Co. will buy the Mill and employ Mr Tulliver as manager. Mrs Tulliver's interference, however, prompts Mr Wakem to buy the Mill, forcing Mr Tulliver into the humiliating position of working for his enemy. Meanwhile Tom, determined to pay off his father's debts, has sought employment at Guest and Co., the firm where his Uncle Deane is a partner. He discovers that his education is useless in the world of business and begins by working in the warehouse and taking bookkeeping lessons in the evenings.

This is an impoverished period for the Tulliver family, both materially and emotionally. Maggie painfully feels the lack of affection from her father and from Tom, both of whom have become preoccupied and withdrawn. Bob Jakin visits with the kind gift of books, one of which has a profound impact on Maggie and she adopts the doctrine of self-renunciation it advocates. When Maggie is seventeen she again meets Philip Wakem, and they continue to meet in secret for a year. When Tom finds out he angrily ends the relationship. Meanwhile Tom's hard work at Guest and Co., plus his trading ventures with Bob Jakin, mean that he can now pay off his father's debts. Returning from the triumphant meeting with his creditors, however, Mr Tulliver meets and viciously attacks Mr Wakem. After this, Mr Tulliver collapses and dies the following morning. Tom promises to care for Maggie and to try to buy the Mill back.

Maggie goes to work in a boarding school, Tom continues to make steady progress at work and lodges with Bob Jakin and his wife, and Mrs Tulliver becomes housekeeper at the Deanes' house after her sister has died. There is a gap of two years and when the story resumes Lucy is on the point of being engaged to Stephen Guest and Maggie is about to come to visit. Philip is close friends with Lucy and Stephen, and Maggie gains Tom's reluctant permission to see Philip again. Philip still wants to marry her, but the intense attraction between Maggie and Stephen complicates the situation.

Tom, although only twenty-three, has been made a partner at Guest and Co. and suggests to his Uncle Deane that the company buy Dorlcote Mill from Wakem. Lucy discovers the plan and enlists the help of Philip who manages to persuade his father to sell the Mill. He also gains his father's permission to marry Maggie. Philip soon becomes aware of the attraction between Maggie and Stephen, however, and at the charity bazaar accuses Stephen of being a hypocrite. At the dance following the bazaar, Stephen kisses Maggie's arm, making Maggie realise the harmful effect of her behaviour on others. She goes to stay with her Aunt Moss, but Stephen visits her and proposes marriage. She refuses, but both acknowledge their love and desire for each other.

When Maggie returns to St Ogg's, Lucy, unaware of the increasing erotic tension between Maggie and Stephen, plans a romantic boat trip for Philip and Maggie. Her plan goes wrong when Philip, so shaken by his discovery of the truth that he cannot bear to see Maggie, writes to Stephen to tell him he is ill. Alone together on the river, Stephen and Maggie drift past the agreed stopping point and Stephen convinces Maggie that they should elope. After a disturbing dream, Maggie tells Stephen she cannot marry him because of her ties to Lucy and Philip. She gets the coach to York by mistake and it takes her several days to get home, at which point Tom disowns her. Maggie and her mother lodge with Bob Jakin. The power of slanderous gossip ends Maggie's short period of work as governess to Dr Kenn's children. She receives a letter from Philip declaring his love for her and a visit from Lucy offering her forgiveness. A letter from Stephen begs her to call him to her, but she resists the temptation. At this crucial point in Maggie's dilemma, the long-threatened flood breaks into the house. As she tries to help Bob to rescue his family, Maggie is swept away. She goes to the Mill to save Tom but their boat is struck by floating machinery and they drown. Five years later we see Philip, Stephen and Lucy visiting their grave.

B OOK FIRST: BOY AND GIRL

CHAPTER 1   We immediately enter the narrator's dream of seeing Maggie Tulliver as he stood on the bridge opposite Dorlcote Mill on a late February afternoon thirty years previously. He wakens from his doze and resumes the story he had been telling concerning the Tulliver family

The novel begins with the narrator's dream of walking along the River Ripple and of seeing Maggie Tulliver outside Dorlcote Mill thirty years previously. The opening description creates a strong sense of setting in terms of time and place. As the narrator's eye moves over the landscape, he describes the distant plain where the Floss meets the sea, and the trading ships which move down the Floss towards the ancient town of St Ogg's. This is an established trading centre located at the confluence of the Floss and the Ripple and surrounded by rich agricultural land.

Wandering along the river the narrator reaches the stone bridge opposite Dorlcote Mill. The Mill is sheltered from the elements by the elms and chestnuts, and is seemingly in harmony with its surroundings. The noise of the full and flooding river and the 'booming of the mill' create a sense of distance from the outside world: 'like a great curtain of sound, shutting one out from the world beyond' (p. 54). He considers that it is time for both the little girl, who is mesmerised by the incessant movement of the mill wheel, and himself to return home. He awakens from the dream and resumes the story he was telling about the Tullivers and what they were discussing on the very afternoon of his dream.

> This first chapter begins some of the central themes of the novel. The first description of the river and sea meeting prefigures the central theme of love and restraint, and hints also at the final tragedy. There is a tension between the emotional 'loving tide' and its 'checking' action, and similarly between the businesslike impatience of the hurrying Floss and the 'impetuous' embrace of the sea (p. 53). Water imagery is central to the expression of deep-seated emotions and desires throughout this novel. The tone of this description is nostalgic, looking back to a golden (pre-industrial) age when human life and work seemed to be in harmony with nature. The 'honest waggoner' returning home, and the harmony of river and mill suggest the central role that the past and bonds formed in the past will have in the novel. One of the most striking features of this opening is George Eliot's use of the self-conscious narrator to tell the story. This is an **omniscient narrator** who will 'intrude' upon the story (see Critical Approaches – Narrative Techniques).

CHAPTER 2   **Maggie's superior intelligence is recognised, but it is Tom who is to be educated. Riley will be asked for advice**

Mr Tulliver has decided to educate Tom so that he can do well in the world. This decision is not entirely without self-interest – he thinks that Tom's 'eddication' will help him to get the better of the law which threatens his livelihood and 'his right to water-power' (p. 58). Mr Tulliver angrily rejects his wife's suggestion that her sisters be consulted.

Mr Tulliver decides to ask Riley for advice about finding a suitable place, and Mrs Tulliver expresses her concerns about being able to care for Tom when he is away from home. Mr Tulliver attributes Tom's lack of intelligence to his Dodson inheritance; Mrs Tulliver does not perceive the insult, but expresses her pride that he has many Dodson traits. Both recognise Maggie's intelligence and both, for different reasons, perceive it as a problem: Mr Tulliver because intelligence is a disadvantage for a woman in the marriage market, and Mrs Tulliver because it leads Maggie to 'naughtiness' and a rejection of feminine appearance. At this point Maggie returns from wandering by the river (as the narrator remembered in his dream in Chapter 1) and uses logic to resist the ladylike activities her mother suggests (p. 61). She is clearly her father's favourite and he colludes in her 'naughtiness'. The closing musings over images of perfect mothers in art carry the suggestion that Mrs Tulliver will have a detrimental effect on her children; here George Eliot juxtaposes the ideal with the real.

In this chapter we first encounter the tensions between Mr Tulliver and his wife's sisters; he resents their interference in his affairs. The Tullivers do not communicate well and neither is interested in the concerns of the other. Much is revealed about their characters from this interaction: Mr Tulliver is blunt and impetuous, much puzzled by the world and by communication, specifically, by the 'raskill' lawyers and the language of the law. Mrs Tulliver is described as amiable but 'dull-witted' (p. 62) and takes her husband's figurative criticism of her tendency to be awkward literally (p. 57). Both speak in a dialect, unlike Maggie and Tom, creating a sense of locality, adding humour and vitality, as well as demonstrating George Eliot's commitment to representing 'ordinary' individuals (see Critical Approaches – Style and Language).

Their discussion begins several thematic threads that will run throughout the novel: inherited characteristics, gender stereotypes, the issue of nature versus nurture, and death. The disparity of educational opportunities for boys and girls is obviously an issue and George Eliot offers a criticism of the unregulated and erratic state of education at this time. The education Mr Tulliver *does* choose for Tom is inappropriate, and clearly Maggie would be far more suited to being 'a bit of a scholard' (p. 56). The way both parents discuss the problems they perceive with Maggie's intelligence is significant: her mother likens her to a 'Bedlam creatur" (p. 60) (suggesting the then contemporary equation between unfeminine behaviour and madness) and articulates the dichotomous conception of women prominent in Victorian literature and art as either angelic or demonic (see Characterisation – Lucy Deane). Her fear of Maggie drowning as a result of her 'wild' behaviour is both a premonition of her death and seems also to be a punishment for Maggie's contravening of Victorian cultural norms (as discussion of witches in the next chapter also suggests). Mr Tulliver, on the other hand, uses a livestock analogy to convey his fears and attitude. This comically undermines his sexist remarks, but also resonates with the evolutionary theme that George Eliot explores in this novel (see Historical Background – Thought and Belief).

be a bread earn a living
Ladyday March 25, feast of the Annunciation
bit o' birch corporal punishment
vallyer a valuer
sanguinary rhetoric bloody talk
put a spoke i' the wheel interfere
'cute acute, clever
Bedlam creatur' an insane person, so-called after the famous St Mary of Bethlehem hospital for the insane in London
mulatter a mulatto, of mixed European-African race
franzy frenzied, cross
Raphael a famous Italian painter (1483–1520)

CHAPTER 3   **Mr Riley advises Mr Tulliver about a school for Tom. Maggie defends Tom's character and shows off her reading and intelligence**

Usually when in the company of Mr Riley, Mr Tulliver would recall the great success of Mr Riley's arbitration about the dam (revealing both Mr Tulliver's preoccupations with his rights over the water and his incomprehension of the law). However, this time Mr Tulliver asks

Mr Riley for advice about Tom's education. Maggie, overhearing Tom's name, immediately leaps to an emotional defence of Tom's character when her father suggests that Tom may want to usurp him in business. Maggie shows off her imaginative and intellectual abilities, immediately detecting the inconsistency in Mr Riley's opinion of *The Pilgrim's Progress* as a book more suitable for girls than *The History of the Devil*. Again Mr Tulliver bemoans the unconventional distribution of intelligence between his children, and reveals that he wants Tom's education to empower him with language to use to his father's advantage. Mr Riley warmly recommends Mr Stelling as a tutor, supposedly on the basis of knowing him well and as a favour to Mr Tulliver. However, as the narrator's comment suggests, his motivation for doing so is complex (see Critical Approaches – Style and Language).

> The narrator introduces the scene of Mr Riley's visit to the Tullivers' house with a sense of immediacy; Mr Riley is portrayed as kindly though a little condescending. Mr Tulliver's admiration of Mr Riley's 'business talents' and capacity to triumph over legal complexities leads to his misplaced trust in Riley's advice. Mr Tulliver's lack of judgement is suggested by his illogical, almost superstitious, attitude to lawyers, and by the fact that he is impressed by the superficial aspects of Riley's character. This trait is confirmed when he reveals that he had literally judged a book by its cover. Following Riley's advice has a bearing not only on Tom's education, but also on the Tulliver family's fortunes, since, contrary to appearances, Mr Tulliver cannot afford one hundred pounds a year for Tom's education. Later, his misjudgement of Mr Riley's business acumen has further financial implications when Riley dies leaving a large debt (p. 274). Mr Tulliver's desire not to be usurped by his son suggests his determination to keep control of his business and to maintain his powerful position of authority in the family.
>
> The simile likening Maggie to a Skye terrier suggests both her unswerving and instinctive loyalty to Tom, and her feisty character (see Theme on Origins and Evolution). Her interpretation of the picture of the witch-dunking reveals a 'no-win' situation for intelligent and unconventional women, who could only gain social acceptance (and prove their innocence) at the price of their death.

This situation clearly has relevance to Maggie and her fate. The cultural conventions that determine this attitude to women are confirmed by her father's hurtful response to her remarks on the devil and by his reason for choosing Bessy as his wife "cause she was a bit weak' in terms of intelligence and assertiveness (p. 68).

had had his comb cut Wakem had been defeated by Riley

Old Harry a name for the devil

Manichaeism an early religious system, named after Manichaeus, which represented God and Satan as equally powerful

Hotspur an impetuous character in Shakespeare's *Henry IV, Part I*

I shan't be … my teeth I won't be forced to give up my power until I'm ready

The History of the Devil by Daniel Defoe (1726)

Pilgrim's Progress by John Bunyan (1678). This book is repeatedly alluded to thematically and in terms of imagery as Maggie makes her secular pilgrimage. See Barry V. Qualls, *The Secular Pilgrims of Victorian Fiction: The Novel as Book of Life*, Cambridge, 1982, for discussion of Victorian literary reference to *The Pilgrim's Progress*

CHAPTER 4   **Because Maggie cannot go with her father to collect Tom from school, she goes to the attic to cry and punishes a wooden doll. She discovers Tom's rabbits are dead but is soon comforted by a visit to Luke's cottage**

Maggie's disappointment at not going to collect Tom is compounded by her resentment of her mother's opinion that it is too wet to go outside. Maggie wets her newly brushed hair in protest and then goes to the attic where she vents her frustration and unhappiness by punishing her doll. Her mood is easily changed by the sight of sunshine coming through the window and she cannot resist going outside. She goes with Luke to the mill and he informs her that Tom's rabbits are dead, a calamity for which she is responsible: 'Tom told me to take care of 'em, and I forgot' (p. 82). She is comforted by Luke's argument that they would have died anyway since 'Things out o' natur niver thrive' and by the invitation to go to his cottage to see his wife, who shows her some pictures (p. 82).

Maggie's punishment of her doll seems to be a direct attack on the feminine ideal that her mother desires for her. Luke's comments about going against nature in the breeding of rabbits also suggest that trying to control natural instincts (Maggie's, for instance) can be destructive. Her mother's comments reveal her concern that Maggie's behaviour will reflect badly on her and her family, and family pride is a factor later in Tom's response to Maggie. George Eliot captures the psychological state of childhood in showing how quickly Maggie changes moods here; she is quick-tempered but easily distracted from her grief. She wants Luke to be impressed by her intelligence and is revealed as highly imaginative. The mill has a special meaning for Maggie and her attachment to it is deep. Her whimsical speculations about the family connections of the spiders reveal her youth, though also suggest the difficulty she feels in fitting into her own family and the pressures on her to comply with feminine ideals of appearance. See Textual Analysis – Text 1. Events have a significant effect on her, as we see in her response to the pictures she sees at Luke's house.

Fetish an inanimate object believed to have magical powers; Fetishism was the lowest stage of evolution in the positivist philosophy outlined by Auguste Comte (1798–1857). The goal of positivism was to create a new social doctrine based not on religious faith and prejudices, but on the laws of science

Jael destroying Sisera in the Bible, Judges 4:7–24. Jael hammers a tent peg into the head of her enemy whilst he sleeps, bringing about a victory for Israel

Pythoness a woman who is believed to be possessed by a god or spirit and who thereby has the power of prophesy; a soothsayer or witch

auricula a species of primula, often powdered white or grey

Pug's Tour of Europe a picture book with doggerel verses on each country (1824)

Animated Nature Oliver Goldsmith, *An History of the Earth and Animated Nature* (1774)

Prodigal Son in the Bible, Luke 15:11–32

Sir Charles Grandison the eponymous hero of Samuel Richardson's novel (1754)

CHAPTER 5   **Tom returns and gives Maggie a fishing rod. He is angry about his rabbits and says she can't go fishing with him. They do go fishing the following day, and their relationship is happy again**

Mrs Tulliver and Maggie both adore Tom, although he is apparently indifferent to their adoration and thinks only of the prospect of fishing the following day. Maggie is thrilled by his gift and proof of love for her, but is soon made miserable by his angry withdrawal of love when he discovers his rabbits are dead. Despite Maggie's distressed state, Tom is cold and cruel, and she is distraught when she goes to the attic. Her mother fears (prophetically) that she has been 'drownded' (p. 90). Just as she is about to go downstairs, Tom, following his father's instructions, comes to find her. The following day they spend a happy time fishing at the Round Pool. Maggie's admiration for Tom and Tom's sense of superiority bring a sense of harmony between them.

We are given a clear insight into Tom's character in this chapter. Although he is described as an ordinary boy, with a 'physiognomy' suggesting only 'the generic character of boyhood', appearances can be deceptive and his strength of character, as well as his inflexibility, is revealed here (p. 84). In saving money for the fishing rods and refusing to be bullied, he proves himself to be kind, brave and honourable, but his strong sense of justice can also lead him to be cold and cruel, characteristics which determine his relationship with Maggie in adulthood. Like his father with his sister, Tom 'meant always to take care of her', but his sense of superiority means that he will 'punish her when she did wrong' (p. 92). Maggie, on the other hand, feels the full consequences of his blame; she longs for love from Tom, but repeatedly does things that make him angry. Their very different temperaments are obvious here.

The Round Pool, 'which the floods had made a long while ago', is a significant setting and captures what seems to be an eternal, idyllic time (pp. 92–3). The narrator's comments at the end of this chapter reveal the inevitability of change, but also that the associations of the place and experiences of childhood have a lasting effect. **Allusion** is made to a Wordsworthian idea of the long-lasting and transforming effect that such interaction with nature can have (see

William Wordsworth's poem 'The Daffodils' or his long poem *The Prelude*, for instance).

physiognomy ... phiz a theory which considers facial features as an indication of personality, popularised at the end of the eighteenth century

CHAPTER 6   **The preparations for the Tullivers' party are underway and there is discussion of the Dodson family traditions. Tom makes Maggie unhappy and goes off with Bob Jakin, with whom he fights because Bob cheats at heads and tails**

Mrs Tulliver expresses concern at the way her children are criticised by her sisters, especially Mrs Deane, and compares their behaviour unfavourably to that of angelic Lucy Deane (p. 96). Maggie and Tom clearly dislike their aunts, and do not behave well, even though they will receive inheritance from them. Again Maggie is upset by Tom when he calls her 'greedy' for eating the best half of the jam puff, which she chose fairly and offered to him. Maggie feels miserable, but is unable to be reconciled with Tom because he goes off with Bob Jakin. Alone, Maggie imagines a perfect life. Tom quickly forgets Maggie in the company of Bob and in the 'manly' discussion of ferrets and a 'rot-catcher' (p. 102). They talk of past floods and Tom plans to make an ark when he's a man in case another flood should come. They fight over a half-penny which Tom wins fairly and Tom returns home.

> The Dodson tradition of 'household management and social demeanour' is described in detail (p. 97). Central to this family's sense of identity is the belief that in all things the Dodson way is superior. Despite this collective self-approval, each sister is critical of the others and Mrs Tulliver is singled out as being a weak Dodson.
>
> The differences between Tom and Maggie are explored further, as is the nature of the relationship between them. Again we see Tom's strong sense of fairness and justice with Maggie and Bob, but this trait also makes him bitterly self-righteous and leaves him isolated. Unlike Maggie, Tom never doubts that he has done the right thing (an element of his Dodson heredity). Maggie again seeks Tom's

approval and would willingly have given up her prize to get it, but Tom refuses her offer. Bob, on the other hand, has a strong sense of personal pride and refuses to hand over the half-penny despite Tom's threats and attempts to gain authority as 'master' (p. 104). The discussion of the possibility of a flood is prophetic, and Tom's plans to be prepared are magnanimous. However, it is Tom who must be grateful to Bob for 'rescuing' him from years of arduous work to pay off his father's debt with his business proposal later (Book 5, Chapter 2).

lief rather

butter-money money earned from a housewife's sale of butter

Rhadamanthine from Greek mythology, Rhadamanthus, one of the three judges of hell, was noted for his sense of justice

CHAPTER 7   **The party begins with Mrs Glegg's criticisms. Mrs Pullet makes a dramatic and tearful entrance. Maggie, compared unfavourably to Lucy, cuts off her own hair. Tom's proposed education is discussed and a disagreement ensues between Mr Tulliver and Mrs Glegg**

The Dodson sisters and their husbands arrive at the Tullivers' house. Mrs Glegg is in a particularly severe and critical mood; the timing of her sisters' arrival and the meal provide scope for her to assert her superiority as a true Dodson. Her hostility towards Mr Tulliver is evident. Mrs Pullet arrives in tears over the death of a friend and Mr Pullet ineffectually tries to defend her in the face of Mrs Glegg's disapproval. The Deanes arrive; Mr Deane is a successful and well-respected business man and Mrs Deane urges him on in his ambition. The friendship between Maggie and Lucy is warm, despite the comparisons made between them, always to Maggie's disadvantage. In her fantasy world Maggie imagines that she is queen and looks like Lucy, but in reality she rebels against such feminine ideals. Because the criticism here is focused on her hair, with Tom's help, she impetuously cuts it off. She wants to be seen as 'a clever little girl' rather than a faulty one (p. 121), but typically she immediately regrets her hasty action. Her father and uncles make light of this incident, but her mother and aunts are horrified. Maggie's father protects her from their 'chorus of reproach and derision', possibly because he understands her impetuosity which is like his own (p. 125). There is general surprise at Mr Tulliver's announcement about Tom's education, but only Mrs Glegg expresses strong criticism. Annoyed by her husband's joking approval, Mrs Glegg is bitterly deprecating about educating Tom 'above his fortin' and about the expense (p. 128). A bitter argument ensues, despite Mr Glegg's attempts to temper his wife's harshness. When she raises the issue of the loan she has made to Mr Tulliver he bursts out with angry insults. Although her sisters try to placate her, Mrs Glegg leaves and Mr Glegg follows her.

> The calculated thrift of the Dodson family and the impetuous generosity of the Tulliver family clash in this chapter. A staunch upholder of Dodson principles, Mrs Glegg is censorious, abrasive and bitterly critical of what she sees as her sisters' extravagance. The Dodson pride is mocked via her rigid opinions on food and appearance; especially comic is her communication of her disapproval through her choice of false hair front and the angle of her bonnet. Aunt Pullet's hypochondria is treated humorously, and her vanity mocked as, even in her tearful distress, she is concerned about her dress and bonnet strings. Susan Deane is the least vocal of the Dodson sisters and her characteristic gesture is closing her lips tightly. Mr Glegg is kindly and humorous, Mr Deane astute and sensible, and Mr Pullet ignorant and ineffectual. Mr Tulliver's sexism is again evident here: he considers Mrs Glegg's outspokenness to be inappropriate for a woman, he directs his discussion of Tom's education towards the men, and is relieved when the women leave the room so that he can have manly talk on superior topics such as business, politics and wars with Mr Deane and Mr Pullet. However, Mr Pullet's stupidity undermines any sense of male superiority. Significantly, we are introduced to Wakem's son here, and anticipate further connection with him since he too is to be taught by Mr Stelling.

> The petty narrow-mindedness of the aunts is representative of the restrictive environment of the St Ogg's community as a whole. Social conventions are rigidly adhered to and respectability is crucial. Maggie's rebellion against such oppression here anticipates

her transgression of social conventions later. The censorious response of her mother and aunts causes her to suffer and, although Tom is 'hard' in his response, he does try to make Maggie feel better with his offer of pudding (p. 123). The narrator's intervention reveals the long-lasting effect of childhood incidents and the use of 'we' encourages the reader to identify with this experience, thus increasing our sympathy (see Critical Approaches – Narrative Techniques).

fronts false hair pieces
Hottentot in Victorian anthropology, South African Hottentots were held to be the lowest of civilisations
Ajax a figure from Greek mythology who in a rage of jealousy kills a flock of sheep, mistaking them for enemy soldiers
Duke of Wellington victor of the Battle of Waterloo (1815), became Prime Minister in 1828
Blucher Prussian general at the Battle of Waterloo
Radicals Liberal Party reformers pressed for parliamentary reform

CHAPTER 8   **Mr Tulliver goes to recall the loan from his sister and her husband in order to repay his loan from Mrs Glegg. His love and sympathy for his sister, and his love for Maggie, lead to a change of heart**

Mrs Tulliver's anxiety about her sister recalling the loan leads Mr Tulliver to visit his sister, Gritty Moss, to recall the £300 loan he made to her and her husband. However, he finds that he can't be as harsh as he intended and having demanded a repayment from Mr Moss, returns to tell his sister he will manage without it for a while.

The importance of money to Mrs Glegg and the Dodson family in general has already been made clear; its importance in the relationship between Mr Tulliver and his in-laws is now stressed. Mr Tulliver is not as rich as he appears, and we learn that Dorlcote Mill is mortgaged for £2,000. He is proud but essentially kind-hearted and generous and, although disapproving of his sister's choice of a husband, loans her money to help with the ever-increasing Moss brood. He sets out, resolved to demand his money back, but softens at his sister's praise of Maggie and when he thinks of Maggie's equally dependent relationship to Tom.

Again we see the incompatibility of Mr and Mrs Tulliver. We also witness the sense of inferiority felt by Aunt Moss because of her poverty. The kindness of Gritty's gift to Maggie, the similarities between aunt and niece, and the good relationship between them (a contrast with the Dodson sisters in all respects) endear Gritty to us and, indeed, to Mr Tulliver. The narrator's intervention against 'Poor relations' seems to encourage the antagonistic feelings towards Mr Moss that Mr Tulliver needs in order to carry out his plan (p. 142). There is **irony** in that Mr Tulliver is later a 'poor relation' too. Following the reversal in his decision, however, he is favourably presented as 'the respectable miller' (p. 144).

father of lawyers a reference to the devil

Markis o' Granby Marquis of Granby, name of a public house

Alsatia a slang term for Whitefriars in London where thieves were out of the reach of the law

CHAPTER 9   **During their visit to Garum Firs, Maggie becomes jealous because Tom favours Lucy. Mrs Tulliver asks her sister, Mrs Pullet, to intervene in the disagreement between Mr Tulliver and Mrs Glegg. The maid brings in 'an object' that makes Mrs Pullet and Mrs Tulliver scream**

While Mr Tulliver is at his sister's house, Maggie, Tom, Lucy and Mrs Tulliver visit the Pullets' pristine home. Before the visit, Maggie is put into a bad temper by the hairdresser, and is hurt by Tom's preference for Lucy and his anger towards his sister's clumsiness. Mrs Tulliver's enjoyment of the visit is enhanced by the opportunity of seeing her sister's new bonnet, which is carefully locked away and ceremoniously revealed by Mrs Pullet. Mrs Pullet's incongruously mournful manner is because she thinks that she may die soon, or worse, that a relative may die which would prevent her wearing her bonnet. Meanwhile Tom has been in conversation with Uncle Pullet, whom he considers to be 'a molly-coddle' (p. 152) and 'a nincompoop' (p. 153). Maggie's clumsiness not only brings reproof from all except Lucy, but also sanctions Tom's resentment of her. Mrs Tulliver has difficulty persuading her sister to help in the disagreement with their sister Glegg , though finally the trivial detail of their similar taste for 'spots' seals their bond (p. 158).

> Tom is revealed to be cold in his treatment of Maggie and cruel in his attack on the bluebottle, 'this weak individual' (p. 147); his fondness for throwing stones at the animals at Garum Firs confirms this cruel streak (p. 148). The way the three children eat their cake is humorously revealing of their characters: Tom is an opportunist, Maggie is a dreamer and Lucy is obedient. Music is enchanting to Maggie, but distracts her and leads her to embarrass and anger Tom, again anticipating later events. Mrs Pullet's excessively protective attitude towards her property and her melodramatic display of her bonnet are comically recounted. Her pride at the number of medicine bottles she has emptied suggests that her illness gives her a sense of achievement, proving her stoicism.

> This visit, simultaneous with that of Mr Tulliver to his family, invites a comparison between Mrs Pullet and Mrs Moss, and between the lifestyles and concerns of the two families. Like Mr Tulliver, Mrs Tulliver is trying to solve the problem of the loan.

Aristotle Ancient Greek philosopher (384–322BC)

Ulysses and Nausicaa they meet in Homer's *Odyssey*

Turkey rhubarb medicinal rhubarb, originally from China

CHAPTER 10   **Maggie has pushed Lucy into the mud. Tom tells on her. Maggie runs away**

The 'startling object' is Lucy, who is covered in mud. Maggie's jealousy is aroused when Tom deliberately excludes her from a forbidden expedition to the pond. Lucy wants Maggie to be included, partly because Maggie would be able to invent stories, an imaginative capacity Tom regards with contempt. Maggie's hurt and anger become too much when Tom tells her there is no room for her to see the water-snake and, to take revenge on Tom via his favourite, she pushes Lucy into the mud. Tom's strong sense of 'justice' requires that Maggie be punished and he tells the maid what she has done, thereby incriminating himself (unjustly, he thinks).

Mrs Pullet, of course, is shocked not by Lucy's distressed state, but by the thought that she might step off the oilcloth. The story only confirms her low opinion of the Tulliver children and again we see Mrs Tulliver's egotistical concern with how this behaviour reflects badly on *her*. On discovering that Maggie is still outside, Mrs Tulliver for the third time expresses her fear that she may be drowned, though this time Tom is included too. This fear is compounded when Maggie is not found by the pond. Mrs Tulliver and Tom leave in the chaise and Mrs Tulliver is anxious to find Maggie, largely because of her concerns at Mr Tulliver's reaction.

> Tom's 'contemptuous conception' of girls (p. 163) is clear here, as is his limited imagination, a crucial difference between him and Maggie. He denies the importance of Maggie's creativity by brutally crushing the earwig, but his own lack of 'imagination', or rather forward thinking, means that he confesses his own disobedience in telling on Maggie (p. 165). He wants only facts and his own interpretation of reality, and he uses violence to maintain his view. However, he is blind to his own wrongdoing and selfishly, like his mother, considers only how *he* is affected by events. Maggie is again in conflict with social convention. The contrast between Maggie and Lucy is stressed, and there are several premonitions of later developments, not least the fact that Maggie inadvertently injures Lucy as a result of feelings of love.

> **Medusa** in Greek mythology, Medusa was one of the Gorgons who had snakes for hair and a look that could turn people to stone
> J4 :X(,2@1 quoted from Aristotle's *Poetics*, meaning greatness
> *corpus delicti* (Latin for 'body of offence') the elements that provide evidence for a breach in the law

CHAPTER 11   Maggie runs away to the gypsies and is taken home by one of them

Maggie's decision to run away to join the gypsies is partly determined by her desire to punish Tom, but also by her romantic imagination and by the fact that she is often told they are her 'kindred' and she longs to fit in somewhere (p. 171). After giving her sixpence to two tramps, she heads for Dunlow Common where she knows the gypsies live. Coming upon a gypsy camp in the lane, she feels flattered by their welcome. Maggie's dream is to be their queen and to teach them 'a great many things' (p. 173). This dream is soon shattered by the harsh reality of their lives, however. She is hungry, but can't eat the 'cold victual' they offer her and they respond 'crossly' to her. She feels lonely and then becomes terrified when two men arrive. Fearing all kinds of horrors, she longs for her father to rescue her. Eventually one of the men takes her home and they meet her father on the way. He pays the gypsy and ensures that the incident is not mentioned at home.

> Maggie's imagination is fired by fiction and her ideas about the gypsies are romantic; this contrasts with Tom's more realistic assessment of them, and indeed of the world in which they live. Maggie's conceitedness is illustrated here, as are the gaps in her knowledge and understanding of the world, and also her contradictory character traits: 'her thoughts generally were the oddest mixture of clear-eyed acumen and blind dreams' (p. 177). Again we see that Maggie, unlike Tom, is prepared to take the blame for her actions.

Apollyon the devil in *The Pilgrim's Progress* with whom Christian battles in the Valley of Humiliation

Catechism of Geography an educational text comprising lists of questions and answers

Mr Greatheart a character in *The Pilgrim's Progress* who functions as a guide and protector

Leonore the eponymous heroine of a macabre German ballad by Gottfried Bürger, 1774, translated by Sir Walter Scott

CHAPTER 12   The mythic and historical past of St Ogg's is outlined. An insight into the Gleggs' marriage is gained and they discuss the loan

The chapter deals with the mythic story, drawn from the narrator's manuscript evidence, of the naming of the town after its patron saint, Saint Ogg. Saint Ogg's courage and understanding of the Virgin's need to cross the river is rewarded and he is said to come again to inspire people in the floods. Against the backdrop of the long historical development of St Ogg's as a trading centre, we are introduced to Mr and Mrs Glegg's 'excellent' house and to their breakfast-time discussion. Mr Glegg is upset by his wife's quarrel with Mr Tulliver and after an argument and reassurance that she would be a wealthy widow after his death, and that the loan is still a good business investment, she decides to let Mr Tulliver have the loan for a while longer.

The gradual development of St Ogg's is informed by George Eliot's understanding of the organic development of society (see Theme on Origins and Evolution). The mythic story of Saint Ogg is significant both in terms of its central message, to meet 'the heart's need', and in terms of the recurrent floods (p. 182).

We are given more insight into the characters of the Gleggs here. Both are preoccupied with money and are miserly, though Mr Glegg is more kindly and genuinely sympathetic for other people's loss; he is described as 'a lovable skinflint' (p. 187). The reference to his tears 'over the sale of a widow's furniture, which a five-pound note from his side-pocket would have prevented' but which he would have considered a 'mad kind of lavishness', is significant for his action later when the Tullivers are in need of assistance. Like Mr Tulliver, Mr Glegg chose his wife for a specific character trait; however, far from the 'conjugal harmony' he envisaged from the union of two thrifty people, Mrs Glegg's meanness of spirit spoils the perfect marital recipe. Mr Glegg, now retired, has two preoccupations: natural history and the contrariness of women.

classic pastorals Greek and Latin poems depicting an idyllic rural past
John Wesley (1703–91) the founder of Methodism, famous as a preacher and writer of hymns
dissenting breaking away from the established Church of England
Harpagons Harpagon is the miser in Molière's play *L'Avare* (1668)
'Saints' Everlasting Rest' Richard Baxter's devotional book, first published in 1650

CHAPTER 13   Mrs Pullet makes an unnecessary visit to Mrs Glegg.
Mr Tulliver writes to Mrs Glegg and obtains a loan
from a client of Wakem's

Mrs Pullet, as promised, goes to mediate in the disagreement between
Mrs Glegg and Mr Tulliver, much to Mrs Glegg's irritation. Infuriated
by what he perceives as his wife's interference in his affairs, Mr Tulliver
sends a letter to Mrs Glegg promising to repay the loan in a month. This
letter only serves to increase Mrs Glegg's hostility towards Mr Tulliver
and to make family relationships worse. Mrs Glegg visits Mrs Tulliver
before Tom goes to school, though expressing her disapproval by
remaining in her gig. Finding no other source for a loan, Mr Tulliver
resorts to borrowing money from one of Wakem's clients.

> Mrs Glegg's attitude here anticipates her later behaviour when the
> Tullivers do become bankrupt: she observes that it will be
> 'wonderful' to her when her negative expectations of the Tulliver
> children come true (p. 196), and also that 'Bessy must bear the
> consequences o' having such a husband' (pp. 197-8). That money
> pressures are likely to increase is implied by Tom's departure for his
> expensive school. The chapter ends with an ominous reference to
> the tragedy of Oedipus. Although, arguably, he is not entirely
> responsible for the consequences, Mr Tulliver's rash behaviour sets
> a chain of disruption in motion.

> **Oedipus** a tragic character in Greek mythology and in *Oedipus Tyrannus*, a
> Greek drama by Sophocles (*c*.496–406BC)

BOOK SECOND: SCHOOL-TIME

CHAPTER 1   Maggie visits Tom at school and is excited by
everything that Tom loathes and struggles with

Tom is shocked by the totally different education he receives with
Mr Stelling. Stelling's method of education and the content of what
he teaches are entirely inappropriate to Tom, whose practical abilities
are ignored. Tom is intimidated by the severity and confidence of
Mr Stelling's teaching and confused by his jokes at the dinner table. The
narrator's digression on meaning and metaphor mocks Stelling's

narrow-minded judgement and limited teaching abilities; the reference to the metaphor of the mind as a 'sheet of white paper' may be a critical **allusion** to John Locke's ideas (see Literary Background).

Tom enjoys taking care of Laura and longs for Maggie's companionship, but is irritated by her knowledge and patronising attitude when she does visit with their father. Maggie is keen to make an impression and be admired for her cleverness, but is 'oppressed' by Mr Stelling's verdict on the cleverness of women as being 'quick and shallow' (p. 221). Tom is relieved to go home at Christmas.

Tom here experiences the mocking humiliation he has inflicted on Maggie and comes to feel 'more like a girl than he had ever been in his life' because of the repeated 'bruises and crushings' to his pride (p. 210). George Eliot comments on the relatively powerless position traditionally allotted to women and the psychological damage caused by feelings of inferiority. Stelling's refusal to 'emasculate' Tom's mind by providing him with a historical context for his learning of Latin is mocked when, as a result of Maggie's questions, Tom does learn better with the help of the 'smattering, extraneous information' usually given to girls (p. 210). This reference to history highlights George Eliot's concern with the impact of an individual's history and memory on the formation of character, and runs counter to the theme of (mis)judging by appearances. The importance attributed to experience and memory is central to the author's call for tolerance and understanding of her characters, and the development of Tom and Maggie needs to be considered in this light. The authority of Stelling's opinion of Maggie's cleverness is significantly undermined by the hostility we are encouraged to feel towards him, and by the narrator's mocking comments. The **irony** of Maggie's exclusion from the classical education Tom struggles with is strong here.

'My name is Norval' from the Rev. John Home's play *Douglas: A Tragedy* (1757)

Massillon and Bourdaloue French preachers renowned during the late eighteenth and early nineteenth centuries

'Swing' and incendiarism during the 1830s, arson attacks were made and threatening letters sent to owners of agricultural machinery in protest against machines that were depriving agricultural labourers of work; the letters were signed 'Captain Swing'

the Eton Grammar   a Latin textbook

Euclid   Alexandrian mathematician and teacher (*c*.300BC)

Delectus   beginners' Latin textbook

calenture   a form of delerium

peccavi   'I have sinned' in Latin

CHAPTER 2   **Christmas doesn't live up to Tom's expectations. Mr Tulliver is irritated about irrigation and Philip Wakem is to be Tom's fellow pupil**

The Moss and Tulliver families gather for Christmas day. Pleasure is disrupted, however, by Mr Tulliver's irritation at Pivart's plans for irrigation upstream from Dorlcote Mill, which he believes will interfere with his water supply. Mrs Moss takes a lively interest in this issue and she and Mrs Tulliver express anxiety about Mr Tulliver's involvement in legal wranglings. These anxieties do not deter Mr Tulliver's determined resistance to this plan, incensed as he is by his suspicion of the involvement of the lawyer Wakem (his long-standing enemy). Here Mr Tulliver's sense of right ('his principle that water was water') is in direct opposition to the law (p. 229). Tom is uneasy when his uncle Glegg informs him that Philip Wakem is to go to the same school, although Mr Tulliver feels proud.

The description of the river is ominous and suggests that the river of life for the Tullivers will not run smoothly for much longer. Mr Tulliver's legal wranglings over the plan to divert the river from its natural channel will have dire consequences for his family. The personification of Christmas as a well-meaning but unthinking being resembles Mr Tulliver. The narrator's comment on the very different effect of this 'fine old season' on the homeless and the poor (p. 223) not only puts Tom's disappointment into perspective, but also **foreshadows** the consequences of his father's rash decisions. The effect of music on Maggie is significant: it fires her imagination and stirs her emotions, though Tom is scathingly critical. The influence of music will be important later in her relationship with Stephen Guest, as will Tom's insensitivity to what affects his sister's behaviour (see Critical Approaches – Patterns of Imagery, Metaphors, Symbols).

'in unrecumbent sadness' William Cowper describing cattle in a winter landscape in *The Task*, V (1785)

CHAPTER 3   **Tom returns to school and an uneasy relationship develops between him and Philip**

Tom's kindness to those weaker than himself is demonstrated in his gift to Laura. This kindness does not extend to Philip Wakem, however, influenced as Tom is by his father's rigid views and his aversion to Philip's physical deformity. After an awkward introduction they do begin to establish a friendship and both demonstrate their strengths to each other – Philip's lie in his intelligence and artistic talents, and Tom's in his physical prowess and courage. Tom is unsure of how to respond to the son of his father's enemy and expresses mean prejudice about Philip's spinal deformity; Philip must restrain his laughter at what he perceives as Tom's stupidity.

Philip's intelligence and sensitivity are contrasted directly with Tom's physical skills and limited imagination. Tom reluctantly admits that Philip is superior in some respects, but is confident that he can 'check' Philip's 'disagreeable points', such as his views on fishing (p. 238). Philip is like Maggie, whom Tom also feels he can 'check' because he is superior.

'Speaker' William Enfield's *The Speaker: or, Miscellaneous Pieces, selected from the best English Writers* (1774), a popular textbook
Richard Coeur-de-Lion Richard I (1157–99), the famous crusading king
bandy hockey

CHAPTER 4   **Tom humiliates Philip. Mr Poulter lends Tom his sword**

The relationship between Tom and Philip continues to be uneven; Tom enjoys Philip's stories and appreciates help with his Latin, but Philip's oversensitivity and Tom's tactlessness cause them to quarrel. For example, in order to counter his 'unmanly' surprise when Mr Poulter draws his sword during a drilling lesson, Tom rushes in to ask Philip to come to see the sword exercise. Hurt and angered by this insensitive invitation to see physical prowess displayed, Philip insults Tom and Tom retaliates. Philip cries bitterly and Mrs Stelling is ineffectual in her attempts to comfort him.

In this chapter the narrator again ironically comments at length on the state of the education system and its inadequacies in giving the sons of businessmen a 'better start in life' (p. 241). Although Mr Stelling's limitations as a teacher are elucidated by comparing him to a rock-boring animal (with a pun on 'boring'), the narrator argues that Tom's experience was luckier than most. Tom bribes Mr Poulter into letting him keep his sword to show off to Maggie on her next visit.

In Mr Stelling's eyes, Tom's stupidity is on a par with a physical deformity, but his own lack of intellectual rigour, his ambition, physique and colouring make an interesting parallel with Tom and his later development. Tom's lack of attention to detail and lack of sensitivity to the landscape confirm the contrast between him and Philip, and also anticipate the compatibility of Maggie and Philip.

Hal of the Wynd hero in Sir Walter Scott's *The Fair Maid of Perth* (1828)

Saladin in Sir Walter Scott's *The Talisman* (1825)

Bannockburn site of a famous battle between the English and the Scots (1314), an account of which appears in Sir Walter Scott's *Tales of a Grandfather* (1830)

divinae particulam aurae from Horace's *Satires*, meaning 'fragment of the divine spirit'

Theodore Hook prolific writer of melodramas, farces and comic novels in the 1820s and 1830s

Bony Napoleon Bonaparte, who died in 1821

General Wolfe English general who secured Canada for England during the Seven Years War

Jupiter ... Semele in Greek mythology Semele was consumed by lightning when she asked her lover Zeus (Jupiter) to appear to her in his true shape

CHAPTER 5 **Maggie visits and Tom injures his foot with the sword. Maggie befriends Philip**

Although Tom acted clumsily rather than maliciously in insulting Philip and his father, the quarrel between the boys is not easily ended. Maggie arrives and is drawn by Philip's intelligence as well as by his deformity since she had 'a tenderness for deformed things' (p. 252). Philip is drawn also to Maggie and he wishes he had a sister like her. He is fascinated with her 'questioning dark eyes' which have an almost magical appeal (p. 253). Tom dresses as the Duke of Wellington and tries to look ferocious, but Maggie only laughs. Tom tries to frighten her, but he drops the sword, injures his foot and faints.

> Maggie is drawn to Philip for the same reasons that Tom is repulsed by him. He satisfies her need both for intellectual stimulation and for expression of affection which Tom will not allow (p. 253). Their relationship later is a development of these feelings, and this early parallel with a brother-sister relationship suggests how Maggie really feels later when ostensibly it has become a romantic relationship. It also brings into question Maggie's relationship with Tom, which is later more intense than either of her romantic relationships with other men.

CHAPTER 6   **Tom will not be lame. A temporary truce is made between the boys. Maggie and Philip become closer friends**

Realising what Tom's fears must be, Philip speaks to the doctor and is able to tell Tom that he will not be lame. Their friendship resumes, Philip entertains him with stories and Tom's sense of pride is restored. Philip wants a sister like Maggie, but is embarrassed by her expression of pity for him. Maggie immediately realises her mistake; she is shown to be sensitive to feelings of inferiority, a result of the family criticism she receives. Maggie wishes Philip were her brother and they part close friends, Maggie promising to kiss him whenever they next meet. Mr Tulliver takes Maggie to a boarding school where she will be with Lucy. The relationship between Philip and Tom soon disintegrates, however, despite Mr Tulliver's advice to Tom to be 'good' to Philip (p. 261).

> Maggie and Philip are alike in many ways, notably in their need for love. Maggie and her father are also alike in their feelings of compassion. The theme of heredity is clear in Mr Tulliver's warning about Philip.

a man who had a very bad wound in his foot refers to Sophocles's hero, Philoctetes, who was abandoned on the island of Lemnos because of his wounded foot; later he helped to bring about the downfall of Troy

CHAPTER 7 Maggie visits Tom at school to tell him their father has lost the lawsuit and is seriously ill and bankrupt

Maggie goes to school with Lucy. Although Maggie always asks about Philip in her letters, Tom selfishly tells her only of his own ailments and activities. She does meet Philip occasionally in St Ogg's, but, now trained in ladylike conventions, she considers it inappropriate to kiss him as she promised to do. A friendship between them seems unlikely when their fathers become involved in a lawsuit. Both Tom and Maggie are growing up: Tom is now sixteen, superficially educated, growing physically and in confidence. Maggie too is maturing and she seems much older than thirteen when she comes to tell Tom the news of their father's loss of the lawsuit and of his serious illness. Both enter adulthood abruptly.

> Tom's self-righteous attitude to Philip reveals again his sense that he does nothing wrong; his inability to perceive the impact that his behaviour has on more sensitive individuals will continue to have a damaging effect. We are told that Maggie grows 'with a rapidity which her aunts considered highly reprehensible', and realise that the unfounded criticism to which she has been constantly subjected continues (p. 263). This increases the readers' sympathy for her. The image of childhood innocence as an Eden-like paradise implies also the inevitability of the fall and division. It anticipates not only the abrupt and harsh entry into adulthood, 'the thorny wilderness' Maggie and Tom experience, but also the Tulliver family 'fall' into poverty and the increasing social divisions which ensue even within their own family (p. 270).

BOOK THIRD: THE DOWNFALL

CHAPTER 1   A flashback reveals what happened to Mr Tulliver

Desperate not to look like 'a ruined man' after hearing of the loss of the lawsuit, Mr Tulliver convinces himself that Mr Furley would buy

Dorlcote Mill and allow him to be the tenant. To prevent loss of their household goods (security for a loan he used to repay Mrs Glegg) he plans that Bessy could borrow money from the Pullets. He writes to Maggie to summon her home. However, he collapses when he discovers that Wakem has the mortgage of the Mill. Maggie's presence comforts him, though he slips in and out of consciousness. Predictably, the aunts feel that Mr Tulliver has got his just deserts; in considering that 'too much kindness' would be 'an impiety', they exhibit the unchristian behaviour Dr Kenn later criticises (p. 279). The following morning Maggie goes to fetch Tom and the chapter ends with a continuation from the previous chapter, with Maggie telling Tom of Wakem's mortgage and Tom vowing to take revenge. He forbids Maggie to speak to Philip.

> It is largely Mr Tulliver's hot-headedness that has brought about this disaster, although his kindness and generosity have also contributed and we are encouraged to sympathise with him. At first he tries to delude himself that he can find a solution, but the shock of reality is severe. The narrator points out that the tragedy of 'insignificant people' is as important as that experienced by the powerful (p. 275). This argument recalls Thomas Gray's eighteenth-century poem 'Elegy in a Country Churchyard', which also acknowledges the experiences and thwarted ambitions of 'common' people. Parallels drawn between Mr Tulliver and animals who fail to flourish after a 'wrench' not only ominously **foreshadow** future events for Mr Tulliver, but also refer to the theory of evolution which informs this novel (see Theme on Origins and Evolution, and Historical Background). The descriptions of Mr Tulliver's nervous state steadily build the tension in the chapter and anticipate his collapse. His childlike response to Maggie mirrors the reversals in their fortunes.

CHAPTER 2   **The bailiff is at the Mill when Tom and Maggie return. Mrs Tulliver is crying over the loss of her things**

Tom and Maggie respond very differently to seeing the 'coarse, dingy man' (p. 280): Tom immediately realises the full and disgraceful meaning of his father's loss; Maggie fears only for her father and rushes to him. They find their mother grieving over the loss of her linen and teasets, in true Dodson manner; finally she is stirred to express emotion but only at the loss of her possessions. That Tom is her favourite becomes blatantly obvious here, and Maggie feels both excluded and angry at the implied reproaches against her father and at her mother's concern for her things. Mrs Tulliver's 'helpless, childish blue eyes' stir a response in Tom (p. 283), much as Mr Tulliver's 'yearning helpless look' stirred a response in Maggie (p. 278). Maggie, having experienced blame all her life, will not blame her father who has always defended her.

> The bailiff sits in Mr Tulliver's chair, a significant invasion of their family life and a symbol of the shame at the heart of their family. For the first time Tom feels reproach for his father and anticipates further difficulties ahead: 'his real trouble had only just begun' (p. 280). His response to Maggie's grief-stricken outburst reveals his cold superiority, though his response to the sight of his father does temporarily heal the divisions between brother and sister. Both siblings are now 'parents' to their mother and father, a sign of the absolute disruption of their family life. Mrs Tulliver's mourning only for her possessions not her husband does seem cold and selfish, but Mr Tulliver's obstinacy and deceit have placed the whole family in jeopardy and blighted forever his wife's girlhood and her past, symbolised in *her* things.

Teraphim household gods, in the Bible, Judges 18:11–31

CHAPTER 3   **The Dodson aunts come to criticise and punish, in contrast to Aunt Moss. Tom's sense of right is shown and Maggie loses her temper**

The consultation with Mrs Deane, the Gleggs and the Pullets does not result in Mrs Tulliver saving her things, as she had hoped. Her sisters, following the Dodson family code, are mean-minded and punitive. Mrs Glegg believes Mrs Tulliver should suffer for the actions of her husband for her 'own good', though this high-minded selfishness is immediately mocked by the narrative comment (p. 290). The sisters bicker and criticise and reveal only their triviality and selfish materialism; Mr Glegg is the first to offer a practical and sensible suggestion. They send for Maggie and Tom, Mrs Glegg believing that they too should suffer for their father's faults. With great effort, Tom proposes that they prevent the sale using his and Maggie's inheritance money, and that he will work to repay the interest. Mr Glegg's admiration leads Mrs Glegg to intervene angrily. The continued bickering and scolding finally become too much for Maggie, who explodes in anger, with criticism ensuing from her aunts. Mrs Moss, guilt-ridden at the £300 debt, expresses genuine feelings of regret and loss and offers to sell their farm to repay the debt. Mrs Glegg's assumption of there being no security offends Gritty's inherent honesty, which is a mark of the Tulliver family. Tom recalls his father's wish that the Moss family should not repay this money and Mr Glegg agrees to help to destroy the IOU note.

> The sisters are cuttingly characterised here: Mrs Deane arrives in her new gig and, although wealthy, she is mean with words and money, as is suggested by her being 'thin-lipped' and having thin hands (p. 287). Mrs Pullet is over-emotional and Mrs Glegg wears her 'fuzziest front', expressing her sense of moral superiority (p. 287). The differences between the Dodsons and the Tullivers are highlighted: the Dodson aunts consider what Maggie asserts as her father's generosity and kind-heartedness to be madness. Mrs Moss's genuine desire to help, despite her inability to do anything financially, also contrasts in every way with the reaction of the Dodson sisters. George Eliot uses much **irony** in this chapter to highlight how little the Dodsons are prepared to do whilst believing they are helping. In Book 1, Chapter 12 she has prepared us for the Gleggs' attitude to charity, and this extends also to Mrs Deane's feeble offer to send jelly and to purchase of some of her sister's best things. The Dodson code of conduct *does* work for the good here, however, but *only* because Tom's (Dodson) sense of duty involves honouring his father's (Tulliver) compassion for his sister.

Homer calls them 'blameless' from the *Iliad*, I
cupped the practice of bloodletting for medical reasons

CHAPTER 4   The legal papers are retrieved from Mr Tulliver's chest;
             he is awakened by the lid banging. Mr Tulliver's
             integrity is evident

As Tom and Mr Glegg retrieve the IOU note from Tulliver's chest, the
lid loudly bangs closed. The familiar sound of this familial chest arouses
Mr Tulliver to consciousness. Apparently with his old force he
questions what is going on and confirms that the note must be
destroyed. Mr Tulliver's recognition of Gritty and Maggie is touching,
and his determination that everyone who is owed money should be
paid is admirable. In particular he mentions Luke's £50 investment.
Mrs Tulliver is 'agitated' by her husband's revival, and he blames
the law for the predicament they are in. His anger at the lawyers and
his worry about his children's future cause him to relapse into
unconsciousness, though Mr Turnbull, the doctor, is hopeful about his
recovery.

> One of the comforts Mr Tulliver has is that Tom's education will
> stand him in good stead. In this, and in his assertion that he is not
> to blame at all, he is mistaken. However, Mr Tulliver's concerns for
> others, especially those most vulnerable, is a redeeming feature of
> his character here.

CHAPTER 5   Tom's visit to Mr Deane is not as successful as he had
             hoped, and he vents his frustration and feeling of
             failure on Maggie

Tom is ambitious and seeks advice from his uncle, who has achieved
rapid success at the trading firm, Guest and Co. Despite Tom's forced
optimism the weather does not bode well. His interview with his uncle
fills him with disappointment; he is made aware that his education is
worthless in business and that he will need to learn bookkeeping and
begin by working in the warehouse. Going out again into the cold and
damp, his ambitious vision of himself as a successful businessman is
now as grey as the thickening mist. Feelings of humiliation are added
to Tom's feelings of failure and resentment when he sees the handbill
advertising the sale of his family's possessions. At home Maggie tries
to help, but Tom vents his anger on her, displaying true Dodson severity
and superiority in showing his 'kindness by finding fault' (p. 319).

Maggie cries bitter tears and longs for love. The narrator compares the extent of Maggie's passions with more famous figures and with the forces of nature. This is similar to the narrator's approach to Mr Tulliver's tragedy in Book 3, Chapter 1.

> Tom is more firmly identified as a Dodson by the publican's comments and by his own thoughts and behaviour. His promise to take care of Maggie provided she obeys him here provokes her tears and we see clearly his complete inability to sympathise with Maggie's feelings (p. 319). Later, this rigid adherence to his moral code has disastrous consequences (as the final paragraph anticipates).

> The weather, beginning 'chill' and 'misty' and 'likely to end in rain' anticipates the dashing of Tom's hopes.

Horae Paulinae *Horae Paulinae; or the truth of the Scripture History of St Paul* (1790) by William Paley

Blair's Rhetoric *Lectures on Rhetoric and Belles Lettres* (1783) by Hugh Blair

nunc illas promite vires (Latin) meaning 'now put forth that strength', from Virgil's *Aeneid*, V

Dominie Sampson ... Lucy Bertram characters from Sir Walter Scott's novel *Guy Mannering* (1815)

Sappho Greek lyric poet born in Lesbos (*c*.610–*c*.580BC); legend suggests she drowned herself for love

Madame Roland (1754–93) wife of a French politician, she was guillotined during the French Revolution

CHAPTER 6   **The sale goes ahead. Bob Jakin comes to the Mill**

The Tullivers remain upstairs during the sale, afraid that Mr Tulliver will be disturbed by the noise. Mrs Tulliver feels agitated about the distribution of her things. After the sale Bob Jakin arrives and recalls the childhood bond he had with Tom. He wants to give Tom and Maggie the money he has earned by his bravery, a gift to reciprocate Tom's gift of a knife years before. He had planned to use it to set himself up as a packman, but he is confident of his luck in earning some more. Tom and Maggie refuse the money, but both are touched by his generosity and concern, and Maggie promises to call on him for help when they need it (as indeed she does later).

> Tom's suspicious response to Bob at first may seem reasonable, given their last meeting, and Tom's 'slight air of patronage' (p. 324) is a modified version of his earlier assertion of social superiority. However, Bob's generosity is genuine and contrasts strongly with the meanness of Tom and Maggie's relatives. Bob is sensitive to Maggie's distress that her uncle Glegg had not bought their books for them, and later tries to compensate her for their loss. In contrast with Tom, he is sure he will be successful in his line of business and is competent in the ways of the world. He embodies a balance of Dodson and Tulliver characteristics in the combination of his shrewd business sense and generous and instinctive emotional response to Maggie's grief (p. 325).

I sarve him out | I take revenge

Do confidence trickster

a big flat a gullible person

CHAPTER 7   **Tom is offered a temporary place at Guest and Co. Mrs Tulliver appeals to Wakem and he decides to buy the Mill**

Mr Tulliver is making steady progress, but is unaware of the full gravity of his situation. Mr Deane gives Tom a temporary place at Guest and Co.'s warehouse and arranges for him to take bookkeeping lessons in the evenings. The Mill must be sold and Guest and Co., considering it a good investment, may buy it and have Mr Tulliver as manager. However, Wakem still has the mortgage on the land and may bid for the whole estate. Mrs Tulliver tries to influence events by secretly visiting Mr Wakem to try to persuade him not to bid for the Mill. Her appeals to his better nature fail and Wakem seizes the opportunity not only to make a good investment, but also to punish Mr Tulliver whilst appearing magnanimous. He is also motivated by the possibility of giving Dorlcote Mill to his favourite son, Philip.

> Mrs Tulliver is motivated by a feeling that her passivity and her belief in her husband's judgement of people have contributed to the

demise of her family's fortunes. However, her naive intervention makes the situation far worse for her family, as her involvement in her husband's affairs has done several times before. Like Mr Tulliver, she overestimates her influence (here an overrating of the Dodson family's importance). The narrator very much guides our response to Wakem. Anticipating the reader's curiosity as to whether Wakem *is* a rascal, as Mr Tulliver says, the narrator points to what seem very trivial and inaccurate assessments of character via his physiognomy (p. 334). However, after the exchange between Mrs Tulliver and Wakem, the narrator's comments confirm Mr Tulliver's assessment of Wakem's character. He is revealed to be devious, cold-hearted and cruelly vindictive. Wakem's enjoyment of his power over Mr Tulliver is expressed in the painful image of 'Tulliver with his rough tongue filed by a sense of obligation' (p. 340). See Textual Analysis – Text 2. This suggests that it is not only Mr Tulliver's actions that offend Wakem, but also his lack of education and his class. His proposed provision for Philip does little to alter our negative view of him, given his mean provision to his other sons.

Allocaturs legal certificates given at the end of a legal action

Hodge a name for an English rural worker

spencer a short close-fitting jacket worn by women in the early nineteenth century

Yellow ... Blue the colours of the Whigs and Tories respectively

CHAPTER 8   **Mr Tulliver realises what has been happening during his illness. He agrees to work for Wakem**

Wakem has bought the Mill and proposed that Mr Tulliver act as manager. The aunts and uncles agree that this is the best solution for the Tullivers and for themselves; they judge Wakem's behaviour as he intended people should. Finally well enough to come downstairs, Mr Tulliver grasps the truth of his situation. In his humiliated state he accepts his wife's reproaches for the first time and, trembling with shame, he agrees to work for Wakem, despite Tom's opposition.

There is great **irony** in Mr Tulliver's mistaken belief in Tom's education as a guard against another challenge from Wakem, given the situation they are presently in. Tom and Maggie's initial response to their father's confusion here is expressed not only in terms of their individual differences, but also in the context of traditional responses for men and women (p. 345). Mr Tulliver's sadness is touching, and our sympathy is maintained for him here.

Saturnalian referring to the Roman feast of Saturn in December where the social order was inverted, the word has become associated with revelry

Nemean Lion slaying the lion was the first of the twelve labours of Hercules

CHAPTER 9   Mr Tulliver comes to terms with working for Wakem. Tom records his father's reasons for continuing at the Mill and his refusal to forgive Wakem in the family Bible

As Mr Tulliver recovers his strength, he struggles to keep his promise to work for Wakem. He is obliged to continue at the Mill due to his dire financial situation, his strong aversion to asking for help from his wife's sisters, and the unlikelihood of finding another position. The most important influence on his decision is, however, his strong attachment to the Mill; inhabited for generations by his family, it was 'part of his life, part of himself' (p. 352). He reminisces about his past and Luke shares his sense of the importance of place. That evening Maggie becomes aware of her father's distracted state; when Tom arrives, he records his father's decision to work for Wakem in the Bible, along with his refusal to forgive him. Mr Tulliver's criticism of Wakem now rings true and Tom, ignoring Maggie's horrified protest, willingly writes that he will take revenge whenever possible.

Mr Tulliver's story of his past 'dropped from him in fragments', mirroring the way that he and the Tulliver tradition are now broken. His description of himself as 'a tree as is broke' (p. 356) reveals, however, that Mr Tulliver sees his attachment to the Mill as an organic connection and one in accordance with nature. His recalling the myth about the river's anger when the Mill changes hands is prophetic, but also makes clear his belief in his right to this place. His wish to bind his son to the recovery of the Mill and to the revenge of Wakem's wrongdoing will have long-term consequences. The familiarity of life at the Mill, likened to the familiar touch of a 'smooth-handled tool that the fingers clutch with loving ease' (p. 352), signals his bond with the past and with the manual craftsmanship soon to be lost to industrialisation.

BOOK FOURTH: THE VALLEY OF HUMILIATION

CHAPTER 1   **A pause in the narrative to reflect on the subject matter and on the traditions and beliefs of the Dodsons and the Tullivers**

Contrasting the ruined castles found on the banks of the Rhine, which recall a romantic, passionate and grandly historic epoch, with the ruined villages on the Rhône, which make even the sunshine 'dreary', the narrator likens the community on the Floss to the latter. Even the tragedy of floods cannot raise the 'angular skeletons of villages' above the notion of human life as 'a narrow, ugly, grovelling existence', just as tragedy on the Floss cannot raise the 'sordid' lives of the Tullivers and the Dodsons above the 'most prosaic' level (p. 362). Their religion is 'semi-pagan' (p. 364), followed because its routines form the centre of social custom and can be used to assert family pride and respectability. Good qualities, such as hard work, honesty and family loyalty, money and pride are at the heart of the Dodson family's beliefs, but so is caring for kin by punishing them (as we saw in Book 3, Chapter 1). The Tulliver family is similar though more imprudent, hot-tempered and generous. The reader is not to be shocked, therefore, at Mr Tulliver recording his vengeful thoughts in his Bible.

In this chapter the narrator engages with the reader directly (we are addressed as 'you') and empathises with the potential irritation a reader may feel with the 'oppressive narrowness' of the subject matter (p. 363). An analysis of the limited and limiting social conditions of St Ogg's gives us an insight into why the Tullivers and Dodsons think and act as they do. We are made aware of the social and imaginative restraint that has such a profound impact on Maggie's development. George Eliot also again offers her analysis in terms of scientific theories of social evolution, arguing that all

things are connected and that each successive generation evolves
to a slightly higher level than the one before it (p. 363). The
angry river, which had caused the tragedy on the Rhône, recalls
Mr Tulliver's reference to the myth that the angered Floss would
flood when the Mill changed hands. Such references contribute to
the developing image patterns that predict such a disaster.

The Valley of Humiliation in *The Pilgrim's Progress* Christian battles with
Apollyon in the Valley of Humiliation, although it is also a fruitful place
Bossuet (1627–1704) French Bishop and prominent seventeenth-century
Protestant
whose breath is in their nostrils recalls the description of the destruction of
the Flood, in Genesis 7:22
fromenty a dish made from hulled wheat boiled in milk
Pitt William Pitt was Prime Minister 1783–1801; the high prices were due
to the war with France and several bad harvests

CHAPTER 2   How life has changed for the Tullivers

At thirteen Maggie is mature emotionally, intellectually and
imaginatively, though she lacks the self-control that makes Tom seem
manly. The monotonous and lonely life she now leads, not having work
to tire and distract her, nor receiving love from her father or Tom, is
making her more introspective. Mrs Tulliver remains 'bewildered' in
her life 'empty' of her possessions, although she shows maternal care
for Maggie by refusing to let Maggie do the heavy work in the house
(p. 368). Mr Tulliver is sullen and taciturn, his previous generosity now
transformed into meanness in his efforts to repay his creditors, whom
he is ashamed to meet. Mrs Tulliver still favours Tom, and Mr Tulliver
still favours Maggie, but has bitter fears that poverty will prevent her
from marrying well. Tom works hard to repay the debts; he becomes
increasingly irritated by his parents.

Poverty and worry have a dehumanising effect, making lives
monotonous and narrowing the scope of discussion and thought
(p. 372). This situation has a highly detrimental effect on the
Tulliver family and the hearth, the central symbol of the home, is
now merely sticks giving out 'cheap warmth' (p. 370).

CHAPTER 3   Bob brings Maggie some books, one of which has a great impact

Accompanied by his canine companion, Mumps, Bob Jakin finds Maggie sitting out in the spring sunshine, though she is not cheered by its warmth. She gratefully accepts his gift of books, and in her lonely and desolate state is profoundly affected by one, *The Imitation of Christ*, written by a medieval mystic, Thomas à Kempis. She responds enthusiastically to its message of self-renunciation and over the next two years she attempts to follow its doctrine. She finds employment and an outlet for her desire for self-mortification in sewing for a local shop, annoying Tom by her indiscretion. Her mother is surprised yet pleased that Maggie is 'growing up so good' (p. 387), but her father only becomes increasingly gloomy that she will not be able to marry well because of his debt (p. 388).

This chapter deals with two years in Maggie's development, as well as commenting on the position of young women generally. Her state of emotional, aesthetic and intellectual deprivation is specific to her and yet articulates also the frustration of many intellectual women of George Eliot's society, who were constrained by social and moral conventions ('the irreversible laws within and without'), and given a very inferior education, if any at all (p. 381). The biblical references underline appropriate behaviour for women: as a moral guide, Maggie is 'Bob's directing Madonna' and he her 'worshipper' (p. 378); but as an intellectually ambitious woman, dissatisfied with her lot, she is the wicked Eve, seeking forbidden 'masculine wisdom', nibbling 'at this thick-rinded fruit of the tree of knowledge' and fearing she may become a 'demon' (p. 380). Believing she has found the key to understanding her life, however, Maggie abandons the 'wrinkled fruit' of other knowledge (p. 387).

George Eliot voices her social criticism through her depiction of the changes in the Tulliver family fortunes. She shows how poverty and distress can have a detrimental effect not only via the lack of material comforts, but also via the psychological and emotional stress caused. Mr Tulliver now has fits of violent aggression and Maggie fears he may beat her mother. The narrator's anticipated

criticism of the realistic subject matter, and of Maggie's religious
zeal, leads to an **ironic** critical assessment which stresses the stark
contrast between the luxury of 'good society' and the hardships
endured by the workforce to maintain it (p. 385). For the 'myriad
of souls' whose lives are physically harsh, religion offers some relief.

Again we see the genuine concern and kindness of Bob, and
class and breeding are wittily discussed in terms of dogs. Though
he could be considered immoral in his cheating, he is not
indiscriminate and takes a logical approach.

Burke's grand dirge a famous speaker and political thinker, his *Reflections
of the Revolution in France* (1790) promoted conservative responses to the
French Revolution; the dirge lamenting the loss of chivalry is from a
passage on Marie Antoinette

Télémaque *Les Aventures de Télémaque* a novel concerned with moral
instruction by Fénélon (1699)

Thomas à Kempis a monk renowned for his piety (1380–1471)

Faraday (1791–1867) eminent physicist who, with Humphrey Davy,
discovered magneto-electricity

BOOK FIFTH: WHEAT AND TARES

CHAPTER 1   **Philip and Maggie meet in the Red Deeps and they
tentatively resume their friendship**

Maggie avoids Philip when he comes to the Mill with his father. Two
days later, he follows her and meets her in the Red Deeps. She enjoys his
admiration, but explains sadly that the hostility between their families
will prevent them from being friends. Agitated and clearly in love with
her, Philip challenges her ideas of self-sacrifice and 'narrow asceticism'
and argues for self-fulfilment and striving to attain one's desires (p. 402).
He tries to persuade her to meet him by appealing to her sense of pity and
arguing that their friendship may heal the rift between their families.
Torn between her longing for companionship and the fear of the
consequences of discovery, Maggie postpones her decision. They discuss
music and she is tempted to accept the book that Philip offers her, but
resists it. Philip knows that Maggie does not feel as he does, but he will

continue to hope that she may come to love him and he will act to protect her.

The Red Deeps represented the farthest boundary of Maggie's childhood experience, and an excursion there required daring and trust in Tom. She recalls her first and lasting memory of Tom holding her hand by the side of the Floss. It is this central bond and her sense of duty to Tom that are put in jeopardy as Maggie tests the boundaries in her resumption of her friendship with Philip. However, it is the more significant moral boundary that she will cross in her relationship with Stephen Guest that finally severs her bond with Tom. Her feelings for Philip are primarily those of pity, not those of love and sexual attraction that the time of year and the secrecy of the place might suggest. Although the 'slow resigned sadness' of her glance makes her seem older than seventeen (p. 393), the narrator comments on 'a sense of opposing elements, of which a fierce collision is imminent' (p. 394). This warns of the conflict she will experience when she is mature and her desire aroused. Here Maggie is firmly associated with a **Romantic** sensibility by her involvement with the Scott novel of frustrated love (p. 401) and by her 'kinship' with the magnificence of nature (p. 393).

Wheat and Tares refers to Christ's parable in Matthew 13:24–30, in which a good man sows wheat, but his enemy comes and sows tares (weeds) in the night; at harvest time the wheat is gathered in, but the tares are burnt

the greatest of painters … divine child refers to Raphael's painting of the Madonna

The Pirate a novel by Sir Walter Scott (1821)

CHAPTER 2   **Bob Jakin helps Tom's career and persuades Mrs Glegg to buy his goods**

As a parallel to Maggie's spiritual struggles and self-denial, Tom has been struggling in the world of commerce, denying himself pleasure and putting his personal ambitions on hold with the aim of first paying off his father's debts. His hard work wins him respect from his aunts and uncles, although he is frustrated by the slow rate at which he can save. A year before Maggie met Philip at the Red Deeps, Bob Jakin had suggested some private trading through a friend of his who travels abroad. Tom was very keen, but his father was not prepared to risk his savings. Bob accompanied Tom to ask his uncle Glegg for a loan. He not only persuaded the Gleggs to loan Tom the money, but with comic effect, also successfully sold goods to Mrs Glegg which she at first snobbishly criticised. A year later Tom has made money and hopes to have cleared his father's debt by the end of the following year; he has kept his success secret, however.

> The contrast between traditional male and female roles and behaviour is discussed in the first paragraph. The usual superior value attributed to the male sphere of action is, however, only equivocally applied to Tom here. This is because in his strong determination to restore a sense of family and personal pride, Tom has become an emotionally cold and closed character. His hard work and success make him feel that he deserves promotion and also engender his resentment of his father's previous actions. The motivation for his silence about his business success is ambiguous and, as the narrator's comments suggest, shows a lack of consideration and holds a possible danger. Again Bob Jakin's personal and business integrity brings hope to the Tulliver family. Both he and Tom are shrewd, although Bob's initiative and generosity mark a distinct difference between them. Bob's manipulation of Mrs Glegg is both amusing and indicative of his skill and of the pleasure he takes in his work.

> **Hecuba, and … Hector** in Homer's *Iliad*, Hecuba laments her son's death
> **Aaron or mouthpiece** Moses's brother who acted as spokesperson for him

CHAPTER 3   **Maggie decides not to meet with Philip again, but is persuaded that meeting apparently by chance would be blameless**

Maggie's mental conflict about seeing Philip hinges on her fear of 'illimitable wants' which may be unleashed as a result (p. 424). Feeling that secrecy would be wrong and that discovery would make the situation worse, she decides to tell him that they cannot meet again. Discussion of his new portrait of her leads Philip to express his discontent with his artistic abilities, which he feels must necessarily be great to compensate for his deformity. Maggie's mention of her method of dealing with her feelings of discontent prompts Philip's criticism. He accuses her of self-delusion, objects to her repression of her imagination and warns of the danger in this (later we see that Maggie's deprivation does have a role to play in her intense attraction to Stephen). He easily persuades her that their chance meetings would not entail secrecy and appeals to her to let him be her 'brother and teacher', although for him the relationship would be far more than this (p. 429). As at the end of Book 5, Chapter 1, Philip wonders whether he has acted purely selfishly, but concludes that he has Maggie's interests at heart. Although the narrator is cynical about the motivations and justifications for his actions, we are encouraged to feel sympathy for Philip because of the physical pain and emotional anguish he has suffered.

> Both Maggie and Philip enter into this new phase of their relationship for similar reasons: partly selfish and partly out of genuine concern for the other. The theme of confinement is articulated here in Maggie's self-imposed imprisonment of her imagination through her renunciation of books, music and intellectual stimulation. Philip's offer of companionship, conversation, books and affection is a tempting freedom to which Maggie silently acquiesces, as later she tacitly acquiesces to 'accidental' meetings with Stephen.
>
> **Hamadryad** tree-nymph in Greek mythology
>
> **the Hunger Tower** in Dante's *Inferno*, Canto 33, where five prisoners starve to death

CHAPTER 4   **Philip declares his love for Maggie and she says she loves him too**

Almost a year has passed and Philip has been lending Maggie books, and acting as her 'tutor' (p. 433). She returns a book to him and criticises the literary convention of the fair heroine always being rewarded with happiness. She responds seriously to his joke about her revenge on the fair Lucy, and her statement that she always takes the side of the rejected lover prompts Philip's indirect declaration of love. She is shocked and responds hesitantly to his question about whether she loves him. With 'sweet, simple, girlish tenderness', she says she does, but uses her anxiety about their relationship being discovered to avoid a definite commitment (p. 435). She is adamant that she will not hurt her father. Philip asks if she loves him only as a brother and her declaration of love is ambiguous: 'It was one of those dangerous moments when speech is at once sincere and deceptive' (p. 437). She kisses him to seal the wish that they never part, but her sense of self-sacrifice rather than fulfilment undermines this romantic gesture.

> The title of the chapter, 'Another Love Scene', draws attention to the previous 'love scene' between Philip and Maggie (Book 2, Chapter 6 entitled 'A Love Scene'); it highlights the fact that although Philip's feelings have changed considerably, Maggie still feels only sisterly affection for him. The discussion of dark and fair heroines not only makes a comment on the literary conventions of the day, but also draws attention to George Eliot's own complication of such simplistic dualities in this novel (see Characterisation – Lucy Deane). It is also prophetic and the reader is alerted to the importance of this by the fact that Maggie takes Philip's teasing seriously. The imagery of the cloven tree bodes ill (p. 436) and the 'flood-marks' of feeling never to be reached again anticipate a decline in emotional intensity in Maggie's relationship with Philip (p. 437). Both suggest the disruption and danger inherent in Maggie's natural feelings, forced as they are here into an increasingly narrow expression.

> **Corinne** a novel by Madame de Staël (1807); the dark heroine eventually dies of grief because her lover abandons her for her fair-haired half-sister, Lucille
>
> **Rebecca and Flora Mac-Ivor, and Minna** the dark heroines in Sir Walter Scott's *Ivanhoe* (1819), *Waverley* (1814) and *The Pirate* (1822)

CHAPTER 5   Tom's suspicions are aroused and he catches Maggie leaving to meet Philip. He argues violently with Philip and then with Maggie

Tom has begun to feel more affectionate towards his sister and even proud of her good looks, but this is soon to be undone. At Sunday tea

Aunt Pullet mentions that she has seen Philip Wakem at the Red Deeps behaving oddly. Noticing Maggie's blushing confusion and remembering their mother recently scolding Maggie for walking in the Red Deeps, Tom becomes suspicious. He determines to discover and end any relationship between them. The next day Bob Jakin sees Philip going to the Red Deeps. Tom returns home and catches Maggie leaving the house to meet Philip. After forcing her to confess what has happened, he gives her an ultimatum to stop seeing Philip or he will tell their father. Although she feels that Tom is wrong, her guilt compels her to give in. He accompanies her to the Red Deeps and cruelly insults Philip, who accepts Maggie's explanation and exasperates Tom with his declaration of constancy. Maggie attacks Tom for his cruelty and accuses him of arrogant self-righteousness, venting her frustration at having no power as a woman; Tom advises her to be submissive. She resents Tom, but she does feel some relief which she attributes to an ending of the secrecy.

> The title of the chapter, 'The Cloven Tree', confirms Philip's fears about the cloven tree; Maggie's relationships with Philip and Tom are both violently split. Tom's intolerance and malicious cruelty is given full vent here, as is his arrogant belief that he can do no wrong. He treats Maggie possessively and wields his (male) power over her mercilessly; he claims he is saving her, but his insensitive action only forces them further apart. The questions that end the chapter suggest Maggie's doubts about her feelings for Philip, doubts that the reader has been aware of from the beginning. This chapter continues the imagery of light and darkness: Tom's 'shining virtues are mere darkness' (p. 450).

CHAPTER 6   **Tom tells his father the good news; Mr Tulliver's thoughts turn to revenge**

Three weeks later, Tom reveals he has made enough money to pay off their debts. Mrs Tulliver responds with an overflow of emotion and Mr Tulliver with stunned silence, which rapidly turns to relief and pride. The creditors are to meet the following day and Mr Tulliver feels triumphant that Wakem will know. Predicting a great future for his son, he asks that Tom try to buy back the Mill in the future. With gratitude and admiration, Maggie feels that Tom's faults have been compensated for as hers have not. That night Mr Tulliver dreams of attacking Wakem.

> Tom's character is redeemed a little for the reader here, although his pride is satisfied as well as his father's. The suddenness of the news, however, precipitates Mr Tulliver's demise and his dream anticipates his actual attack on Wakem.

CHAPTER 7   Mr Tulliver has a moment of triumph as he meets and pays his creditors. He attacks Wakem and dies the following morning

At the meeting with his creditors Mr Tulliver looks and acts increasingly like his old self. Tom makes 'the single speech of his life' (p. 459) and Mr Tulliver boasts of his son's education. Riding home, Mr Tulliver broods on the fact that he has not seen Wakem. His simmering resentment reaches boiling point when he meets Wakem coming out of the Mill gates and Wakem patronisingly criticises his work and dismisses his anger as drunkenness. Causing Wakem to fall from his horse, Mr Tulliver beats him with his riding whip and is only stopped by Maggie. Wakem rides home accompanied by Luke, and Maggie and Mrs Tulliver help the now faint Mr Tulliver inside. Tom returns and feels frustrated that his hard work must always be confounded by the actions of others. In contrast, Maggie is haunted by her experience. During the night Mr Tulliver's condition worsens. He repeats his request that Tom try to buy back the Mill, and also instructs him to take care of Maggie. He still does not forgive Wakem and his final words reiterate his confusion at the changing world he has lived in. Maggie calls for Tom's forgiveness and they weep together.

> The violent swing from celebration to disaster seems melodramatic, but the events in this chapter have been clearly anticipated: the danger of the news coming too suddenly for Mr Tulliver (Book 5, Chapter 2, p. 423 – Tom might have acted to 'prevent the delerium of a too sudden elation') and the possibility of his violent and 'disgraceful' behaviour (Book 4, Chapter 3, p. 373). The 'long-smothered hate' that Mr Tulliver feels for Wakem (p. 462) has been a constant feature, as has the trouble caused by his impetuous

nature. Tom's self-pitying reflection that his life is inextricably bound up with others and their misdemeanours refers again to the idea of a web that forms connections between individuals (see Critical Approaches – Characterisation, and Theme on Origins and Evolution). For Tom 'the mingled thread in the web of their life' which is 'so curiously twisted together that there could be no joy without a sorrow coming close upon it' is a regrettable thing, not one that increases his tolerance of others (p. 462). His promise to care for Maggie is later broken, or at least not fulfilled in the generous spirit with which Mr Tulliver intended.

BOOK SIXTH: THE GREAT TEMPTATION

CHAPTER 1   Lucy and Stephen discuss the arrival of Maggie

It is two years since Mr Tulliver's death and Maggie has been working in a school in order to maintain her independence. Lucy's mother is also dead and Mrs Tulliver has been acting as the Deanes' housekeeper. Maggie is to come to stay. To tease Stephen, Lucy confirms his expectations that Maggie will resemble her mother. Philip is a friend of theirs and Lucy tells Stephen of the tension between the Wakems and the Tullivers. She will ask Philip to wait until she has spoken to Maggie before he visits again. Lucy and Stephen sing together and Stephen leaves for lunch. Lucy, fond of pandering to dependent creatures, takes her dog with her to feed her horse.

> Lucy, 'angelic' and 'faery', conforms to the Victorian ideal of femininity. The narrator stresses her goodness which finds an outlet in the treats she has planned for Maggie and her aunt Tulliver, paralleled here with her indulgence of her pets. The courtship between Lucy and Stephen has not been formalised and, although there seems no doubt about it going ahead, the narrator's comments add a sense of uncertainty. The fact that music is said to seal the bond between lovers, here Lucy and Stephen, also anticipates the attraction of Maggie and Stephen, who are similarly drawn together through music. The title of the chapter, 'A Duet in Paradise', and the duet that Lucy and Stephen sing make reference again to Adam

and Eve's Fall. Already such biblical echoes have been associated with Maggie's unfeminine craving for education; now they are repeatedly associated with a desire for sexual knowledge which will similarly bring about a fall from innocence and social acceptability.

The presentation of Stephen is not sympathetic: he is a large and striking young man, but one who has a cruel streak, seen as he snaps the scissors in Lucy's dog's face. He is also patronising to Lucy and dismissive of the business which has made him a gentleman. His choice of Lucy for a wife is driven by his conventional tastes and, as the narrator comments, he is not perceptive enough to recognise Lucy's 'rarest quality', which is her ability to genuinely love and care for other women (p. 477). This is very significant later, to explain his lack of understanding not only of the tremendous forces acting on Maggie when she betrays Lucy, but also of Lucy's response. He is of great importance in Lucy's 'small world' (p. 476), but the final sentence of the chapter again suggests a note of ambiguity. The whole scene reminds the reader of Philip's teasing suggestion that Maggie should be a rival to Lucy and win 'some handsome young man of St Ogg's' from her (p. 433).

da capo a musical notation meaning from the beginning
Beatrice in the *Vita Nuova* and *The Divine Comedy* Dante celebrates his love for the idealised Beatrice
The Creation by Haydn (1798)

CHAPTER 2   Maggie and Stephen meet. Lucy, Stephen and Maggie go rowing

Discussing Stephen with Maggie, Lucy expresses her fears and insecurities about marrying him. They discuss Maggie's hard life experiences and Maggie contrasts her own bitterness and jealousy with Lucy's pleasure in seeing others happy. Lucy is confident that she can make Maggie happy with music and mentions that Philip Wakem sings with them. Before Maggie can explain her relationship with Philip, Stephen arrives and is immediately fascinated by Maggie's appearance, intelligence and defiance, and by her impoverished circumstances. Maggie is flattered and his discussion of books, especially one dealing

with new scientific theories, attracts her attention. He criticises Maggie
to Lucy, but we are aware that he is attracted to her. The three of them
go rowing and return home to find that the Pullets have arrived. Stephen
hurries away, but will return that evening. Discussion of clothing for
Maggie leads to criticism of her large brown arms. Lucy immediately
defends her cousin, again expressing her admiration for Maggie's
appearance. Uncle Pullet's reference to the 'Nutbrown Maid' hints at the
issue of fidelity.

> In this interaction between Lucy and Maggie the difference in
> their appearance is highlighted – 'aerial' (p. 480) and 'dark lady'
> (p. 479) – as are their different experiences and outlooks on life.
> The dialogue also establishes their warm affection for each other
> and their mutual trust. Maggie's hardship has left her full of
> longings and desires. In these circumstances the 'riotous feast' (p.
> 483) of music which Lucy offers will be precisely the excessive
> temptation Maggie will be unable to resist, accompanied as it is
> by the romantic and sexual temptation of Stephen. Mention of
> the altruistic goodness of Dr Kenn and Maggie's admiration of
> this quality is significant later. The narratorial comment
> engages **ironically** with Stephen's self-deceptive justification of his
> attraction to Maggie and of the unimportance of this attraction. His
> state of being 'half engaged' (p. 491) to Lucy, plus Maggie's joking
> comment that Lucy could easily give Stephen up since they are not
> engaged, serve to highlight the uncertainty of the relationship.

> **Buckland's Treatise** William Buckland's *Geology and Mineralogy Considered
> with Reference to Natural Theology* (1836)
> **'Nutbrown Maid'** a fifteenth-century ballad about female fidelity
> **crazy Kate** in Cowper's *The Task*, I (1785), Kate goes mad when her lover
> abandons her

CHAPTER 3   **Maggie tells Lucy of her relationship with Philip
and Lucy proposes to give it a 'fairy tale' happy
ending**

After an evening of music and 'furtive' attention from Stephen, Maggie
is too excited to sleep. Lucy comes to her room eager to know Maggie's

opinion of Stephen. Lucy's news that Philip will come the following evening prompts Maggie to explain why she must have Tom's permission to see Philip, though she omits the worst offences that Tom and her father have committed against the Wakems. Lucy claims she will act as matchmaker for Maggie and Philip, and Maggie's shiver at the thought is telling. The final sentence continues the ambiguity associated with Maggie's romantic attachments.

Attention is drawn to Maggie's lack of experience, to her 'hungry nature' (p. 494) exacerbated, as Philip earlier predicted, by self-renunciation, and to her desperate need for an outlet for her imaginative, intellectual and sensual capacities. The reader is aware, however, that it is not just the 'provincial amateur' musical performance that has so profound an impact on her emotions; her sexual appetite has also been stimulated. Lucy expresses her admiration of Maggie's intelligence here in terms of 'witchcraft' (p. 498), as earlier she referred to Maggie's attractiveness as 'witchery' (p. 480). This continues the angel–witch dichotomy, which builds a sense of foreboding given what we have heard about the fate of witches and what we know of the literary conventions of the period (p. 66, p. 433). It ominously suggests Maggie's potential for what would conventionally be perceived as wickedness.

Sir Andrew Ague-cheek a comic figure in Shakespeare's *Twelfth Night* who claims 'I was adored once, too' (II, ii)

CHAPTER 4   **Maggie visits Tom at Bob Jakin's house. Tom reluctantly agrees to let Maggie see Philip**

Bob Jakin, now married, lives with his wife and his mother in a house by the side of the Floss. Maggie is saddened by Tom's reduced circumstances and surprised to discover that Tom has worries too. Bob expresses concern about Tom's solitariness and there are hints that Tom may be in love with Lucy, though Maggie is not convinced. Tom coldly consents to her request to be allowed to see Philip, though he will disown her should Philip become her lover again. He accuses her of being inconsistent and lacking good judgement. She can see that to a certain extent he is right, but rebels against his total lack of understanding of her.

Maggie reminds him of her obedience to his wishes, and his desire to protect her eases the hostility and they part friends.

> There are many touches of humour in this chapter concerning Bob's marriage, not least the fact that Mumps's 'opinion' is still central. The vast difference between Maggie and Tom is as great as ever and is revealed in the strained interaction between them here. Tom's conventional assumption that as a man he knows best and that women need to be treated and cared for like children (humorously mirrored in Bob's choice of a diminutive woman for his wife) merely emphasises his limited understanding and antagonises Maggie further. Paradoxically, in treating her as a child, he arouses a childlike response in Maggie and her simple needs are expressed with the daisy simile (p. 503), although Tom is unable to respond with affection. It is, however, Maggie's behaviour as an independent woman that arouses his antagonism, contradicting as it does his conventional beliefs of appropriate roles for men and women. To Maggie his disapproval and criticism seem 'prophetic … predicting her future fallings' (p. 504), and we see that he is right to some degree. There are several hints about Tom's love for Lucy, which may help to explain his brooding bitterness, especially given his rival's mocking attitude to his success in business (p. 473–474).

CHAPTER 5   **Tom is offered a share in Guest and Co. and asks that they buy Dorlcote Mill and appoint him as manager**

That afternoon Tom meets with his Uncle Deane. After some discussion of the fast pace of business and life and his self-congratulation at being right about Tom, Mr Deane announces that Tom's seven years' hard work is to be rewarded with a share in the business. Tom broaches the subject of buying back Dorlcote Mill, as his father wished, stressing his preference for this over any better opportunity. Mr Deane is sympathetic to Tom's proposal to manage and eventually buy the Mill, but is uncertain whether Wakem will sell it. Tom is optimistic and they will discuss it further when Tom returns from his business trip up north.

> Steam and industrialisation have speeded up the pace of life and this is mirrored in Tom's rapid success. Mr Deane's fatherly

admiration of Tom's astute business sense helps to highlight his misgivings about his future son-in-law's lack of interest in business, although he clearly admires Stephen's eloquence. Even the 'business-loving ears' of Mr Deane are saddened, however, by Tom's sole interest in work (p. 511). The chapter title, 'Showing that Tom Had Opened the Oyster', marks Tom's progress – the 'oyster' of Book 3, Chapter 5 ('Tom Applies His Knife to the Oyster') is now open. The complications in the purchase of the Mill are anticipated here.

CHAPTER 6   The relationship between Maggie and Stephen develops

Maggie's striking looks and style of dress are admired by both the women and the men in 'the higher society of St Ogg's'. She revels in the luxury of this life and in the attention she receives, especially from Stephen. In the twelve days that Philip is away on a sketching expedition the erotic tension between Maggie and Stephen increases. Lucy is unaware of this and her suspicions would, in any case, have been deflected by Stephen's increased attention to her. One evening Lucy goes to visit Mrs Kenn and Stephen calls on Maggie unexpectedly on the pretext of bringing Lucy some music, though the music is soon neglected. Both are embarrassed and focus on the dog, Minny, to avoid making eye contact. Eventually Stephen leaves, and Maggie accompanies him into the garden. Back in the house alone, Maggie longs for the safety and innocence of being back in the Red Deeps with Philip. Stephen smokes all evening determined not to think; he is both conscious of and annoyed by the intense attraction he feels for Maggie.

> The season, 'advancing Spring', and the sensual experience of luxury have an 'intoxicating' effect on the inexperienced nineteen-year-old Maggie (p. 513). Music excites her, it is a 'pregnant, passionate language to her' and an outlet for her 'passionate sensibility' (p. 513); it is also a metaphor for her sexual feelings. She is clearly predisposed to a heady sensual response, though George Eliot is careful to make clear that it is not only character that dictates one's future – chance plays a crucial role in destiny too (ominously the tragedy of Hamlet is used to illustrate this). The narrator's use of

questions highlights the fact that Maggie and Stephen do not want to question what is happening, and the sensuous imagery and the displacement of Stephen's attention to Minny's dark hair make the sexual attraction between them obvious. The river imagery used to describe Maggie's destiny as uncertain and yet ultimately predictable (all rivers end in the sea) contributes to what have been largely foreboding references to the river; it seems no coincidence that Stephen comes on his illicit visit via the river.

Novalis the pen-name of German poet and novelist Friedrich von Hardenberg (1772–1801)

Miss Sophia Western heroine of Henry Fielding's *Tom Jones* (1749)

Maid of Artois (1836) an opera by Michael William Balfe

CHAPTER 7 **Philip visits Maggie and Lucy. Stephen arrives. Lucy talks to her father about Guest and Co. buying Dorlcote Mill**

The visits of Philip and Stephen are preceded by a mocking assessment of men's attitude to visiting and to women which implicates them both. Philip arrives and his restraint contrasts with Maggie's warm welcome; she cries tears of happy relief and hopes that he may save her from the temptation of Stephen. Although they are soon affectionate again, Philip detects a change in Maggie. When Stephen arrives they play and sing. The music has a mesmerising effect on Maggie and her open response is alluring to all. Her different responses to the songs sung by Philip and Stephen is revealing (see Critical Approaches – Patterns of Imagery, Metaphors, Symbols). Maggie is flattered by Stephen's attention and Philip, predisposed to be suspicious and jealous, immediately suspects the truth. Mr Deane's questions to Philip about his father's business prompt Lucy to later discover the plan to buy Dorlcote Mill, and she resolves to enlist Philip's support.

> The contrasting behaviour of Maggie's two admirers, plus her response to them, helps the reader to accept her preference for Stephen. Although an honourable man, Philip's oversensitivity reduces our sympathy for him here as he vents his bitterness in his criticism of Maggie, and reproaches her with his choice of song. As with Tom, Maggie assumes a childlike response to Philip's

chiding of her, whereas with Stephen she expresses more mature emotions. Maggie's guilty feelings surface when she recalls Philip's earlier teasing about stealing Lucy's lover (p. 529). Despite the determination of both Stephen and Maggie to be indifferent to each other, the attraction between them is too great. Music stirs Maggie's intense emotions and water imagery expresses the danger of her loss of control (as later the river will literally carry her away). Their attraction is a force beyond their control and beyond the bounds of civilised society.

Masaniello Daniel F.E. Auber's opera (1828)

Let us take the road a chorus in John Gay's *The Beggar's Opera* (1728)

Sonnambula opera by Vincenzo Bellini (1831)

Shall I, wasting in despair George Wither from *Fair Virtue* (1622)

The Tempest music for the songs in Shakespeare's play composed by Thomas Arne in 1746

CHAPTER 8   **Philip persuades his father to give his consent for him to marry Maggie. Wakem also agrees to sell Dorlcote Mill**

After talking to Lucy, Philip resolves to speak to his father about Maggie and about Dorlcote Mill. He invites his father to his studio where he has displayed his two portraits of Maggie. At first his father is angry to hear of Philip's attachment to her, but, by playing on his father's feelings about his deformity, Philip gains both his father's consent to marry her and his agreement to sell the Mill. Their discussion ends with a touching resumption of the close bond between beloved son and widowed father, and the following day Philip tells Mr Deane the news.

As the title, 'Wakem in a New Light', suggests we see Mr Wakem from a different perspective: he is revealed to be an affectionate, loving and devoted father and a devoted husband. We also see Philip manipulating others in a more cool and calculating way than before. His anger over his father's view of Maggie as an object belonging to the Tulliver men reveals the depth of his love for Maggie and his need to separate her from those who have prohibited his relationship with her. Philip's dream about Maggie's fall into a watery grave is full of foreboding, not only anticipating the ending of the novel, but metaphorically suggesting his inability to save her from her fall into sin when she rows away with Stephen.

CHAPTER 9   At the Bazaar, Philip accuses Stephen of hypocrisy and Maggie tells Lucy that she has a new position

At the Bazaar Maggie's beauty and simplicity of dress allure men to her stall, amongst them Philip's father who acts with tact and sensitivity. Whilst other women envy Maggie, criticise and compete, Lucy feels only admiration and excitement at the prospect of finally uniting Maggie and Philip. Stephen offers Maggie some refreshment and, alerted to the fact that Philip is watching them from the orchestra space, he begins to suspect that the relationship between Maggie and Philip goes beyond friendship. Stephen's exchange with Philip is bitter and Stephen is frustrated by his situation. Meanwhile Dr Kenn, noticing Maggie's unhappiness, speaks to her kindly and offers her help should she need it in the future. Lucy is hurt and shocked when Maggie tells her she is leaving to take up a new position. Although Lucy gives her the opportunity to be honest about her feelings for Philip, Maggie maintains that it is only Tom's objection that prevents her from marrying him.

> Both Maggie and Stephen are envied by members of their own sex, but it is the 'feminine judges' of St Ogg's whose opinion will be so damaging to Maggie later. Stephen, on the other hand, will be judged more tolerantly, although despite the narrator's assurance that Stephen 'was not a hypocrite' but experiencing 'a moral conflict', we have doubts about him (p. 552). The harsh public opinion of Maggie is countered here and later by Dr Kenn's perceptive kindness and his pity for those 'strugglers still tossed by the waves' (p. 553). Again river imagery expresses Maggie's conflict between desire and duty, as well as her wish to escape (p. 555). The music of Stephen's voice, 'like a sudden accidental vibration of a harp close by her' (p. 551), suggests the sexual tension between them. By contrast, Philip watches Maggie from the empty orchestra space. The attraction between Maggie and Stephen is likened to an opium addiction, suggesting both the uncontrollable and unhealthy

nature of this, and the social disapproval that will ensue when it is known.

frosty Caucasus in Shakespeare's *Richard II* (I, iii)

the giant Python a mythical creature killed by Apollo in Greek mythology

The souls by nature ... from John Keble's *The Christian Year* (1827)

CHAPTER 10   Maggie attends the dance at Park House where Stephen kisses her arm. The following day she confirms her feelings for Philip

Despite her resolution not to dance, Maggie is unable to resist the music, and Stephen's jealousy is aroused by her dancing with someone else. Breaking his resolution, he speaks to her and they walk to the conservatory, where the unrealistic romantic setting and the thought that this will be their final meeting bring Stephen's desire to the surface. Overcome with passion he is unable to resist kissing Maggie's arm as she reaches to pick a rose. The narrator's comment attempts to offer mitigating evidence against Stephen's crime. However, Maggie is shocked into realising her treachery against Lucy and Philip and the injury to her own self-respect. She now feels purged of her desire and able to fulfil her duty. The following day, feeling completely in control of her emotions, she assures Philip that only Tom's disapproval would prevent her from marrying him. However, Philip, like the reader, is not entirely convinced and, as the chapter title suggests, the spell only 'seems' broken.

The music that stirs Maggie's passionate response and breaks Stephen's resistance has a 'half-rustic' rhythm (p. 559); it significantly blurs the categories of town and country and what they represent – cultured or civilised responses and more natural instinctive ones. Stephen's sexual desire is expressed with reference to the life-preserving instincts of hunger and 'thirst' (p. 559), whereas Maggie's 'hunger' for the smell of the (highly symbolic) rose is described as 'wicked' (p. 561). In the 'enchanted land' of the conservatory Stephen's senses are blurred in the powerful confusion of his desire (p. 560). All the conventional **tropes** of romance and sensuality are used to build up the overpowering sense of desire between them; this is shattered when the desire is acted upon, however. Maggie's reaction to Stephen's kiss is a moral one, but one based on her personal morality which is bound up with the past and with connection to others. This morality is an important factor in her refusal of Stephen in the chapter that follows.

the enchanted cup in Milton's *Comus* (1634) the Lady is saved from Comus's temptations by the arrival of her brothers

CHAPTER 11   Stephen visits Maggie at her Aunt Moss's house. She refuses his proposal

Four days after Maggie's arrival at her Aunt Moss's house, Stephen arrives and insists that they walk together. He confesses the extent of his feelings for her and begs her to marry him, trying to persuade her that their commitments to Lucy and Philip are 'unnatural' and false. However, although tempted, Maggie refuses to attain happiness by sacrificing others. Although Stephen 'had the fibre of nobleness in him', he is also overcome by his desire and requests a kiss from Maggie (p. 571). After this, Stephen leaves and Maggie is comforted by her aunt.

The river imagery here expresses the ease and pleasure Maggie would experience in giving in to her desires, in letting herself be swept along by the 'current', which is 'soft and yet strong as the summer stream!' (p. 569). However, this surrender would conflict with her sense of duty to others, as it does later when she literally drifts down the river with Stephen. Both Maggie and Stephen agree that their love is 'natural' and Maggie imagines 'paradise' as being when two people who love each other could be free to be together. However, unlike Stephen Maggie sees also that faithfulness, pity and memory are natural too, and that loyal ties with others are at the heart of moral goodness and duty. This argument is reiterated more forcefully in Chapter 14.

CHAPTER 12   A family party is held to celebrate the purchase of Dorlcote Mill. Lucy's plan to heal the Wakem–Tulliver rift fails

The Pullets hold a party to celebrate the Tullivers' acquisition of the Mill and Lucy tactically encourages her aunts to give some of their linen to

Aunt Tulliver and Tom. Aunt Glegg is as stern as usual and demands dutiful respect from Tom and Maggie, as a mark of which she expects Maggie to come and sew for her. Aunt Pullet is fussy and scathing of her sister's taste. Mrs Tulliver is keen to maintain her innocence with regard to Maggie's decision to work. Lucy tells Tom of the part Philip played in persuading his father to sell the Mill in the hope that he will view the relationship between Maggie and Philip more favourably. However, this only serves to arouse Tom's prejudices further and leads him to question how far he can trust Maggie.

> Mr and Mrs Pullet and Mrs Glegg are subject to mockery here and only Mr Glegg seems capable of feeling genuine happiness at Tom's success. They are all critical of Maggie's desire for independence, but their own eccentricities make Maggie's decision seem all the more reasonable. Tom's predisposition to hold deep-seated prejudices is confirmed here and the intensity of his prejudice against the Wakems is explained – it has become 'a meeting-point' for his sense of injured personal and family pride (p. 579). This clear description of his character prepares the reader for his attitude to Maggie's truly 'perverse' behaviour later. His rigid adherence to his conventional 'upright' views and his prejudices will similarly be the 'staff' with which he justifies his treatment of Maggie and the 'baton' with which he punishes her (p. 579).

CHAPTER 13   Stephen rows Maggie beyond the meeting point with Lucy. He proposes that they elope to Scotland and they are taken on board a passing trade steamer

After her return to St Ogg's, Maggie spends her days with her Aunt Glegg, but returns to dine with Lucy. Despite some effort to remain away, Stephen is unable to resist being in Maggie's company while he can. Lucy attributes Maggie's depressed mood to her being torn between Tom and Philip; little does she realise the emotional and moral struggle Maggie is experiencing. Lucy's scheme of sending Philip and Maggie boating alone together fails because Philip, agonised by what he rightly suspects is the relationship between Maggie and Stephen, is too ill and unsure of his motives to see her. His note to Stephen saying he is too ill to row, and Lucy's preconceived plan to go shopping at the last minute, mean that Maggie and Stephen are left alone together. After some reluctance on Maggie's part they go rowing. The weather and the motion of the river seem to be benign omens, an 'enchanted haze' creating a sense of suspension from real life (p. 589). They go a long way past Luckreth, where they were to have stopped and met Lucy, and Stephen tries to persuade Maggie to elope to Scotland. At first Maggie is shocked and angry, but when she realises that Stephen had not planned this and would take all the blame himself, she becomes 'paralysed' and then can only yield to Stephen's will. They persuade a Dutch steamer to take them to Mudport and Maggie falls asleep, but with a sense that 'the morrow must bring back the old life of struggle' (p. 595).

> Maggie's moral and emotional turmoil is stylistically conveyed, especially in the second paragraph, by George Eliot's use of fragmented sentences, question marks and exclamation marks. Stephen's innermost desires and his longing to hold on to Maggie are unconsciously betrayed through music. Maggie's longing to give in to the flow of her emotions is expressed with the suggestion that the flow of the river is an agent directing her fate. The moral danger she and Stephen are in, however, is metaphorically suggested by their drifting down the river and by the change in the weather. On board the steamer Maggie experiences her moral passivity and abdication of responsibility as 'a soft stream' flowing over her (p. 595).

The thirst ... divine Ben Jonson's poem, 'Song to Celia', from *The Forest* published in 1616

CHAPTER 14   **Awakening, Maggie realises that she must return home. By mistake she takes a coach to York**

Though distracted by thoughts of the future, Stephen eventually falls asleep. Waking from troubled dreams, Maggie considers her actions and feels guilty remorse for how they will affect those she loves. Torn between not wanting to cause Stephen pain and her sense of duty, Maggie waits until they are almost at Mudport before telling him of her resolve to leave him. At the inn Stephen tries desperately to persuade her to continue with their plan. He argues, as he did earlier in the lane, that their mutual love and attraction are natural and that their marriages to others would be 'hollow', and also that they have already caused Lucy and Philip pain (p. 602). However, for Maggie their life would be embittered by the pain caused to others and, despite his accusation that she has betrayed him, she leaves. She catches a coach to York by mistake and spends a night at an inn, disturbed by dreams and a deep sense of the loss of love.

> Maggie's first dream is double layered: the first layer echoes the mythical story of St Ogg's with the protagonists significantly changed to those whom she feels she has wronged. Reaching out in her dream she causes her own boat to sink and she slips into the second layer of her dream, recalling her childhood bond with Tom. With her 'real waking' Maggie realises the 'terrible truth' as she also awakens morally to what she has done (p. 596). These dreams anticipate her reunion with Tom and their death, as well her wish for him not to be angry with her. The 'web' metaphor is used to suggest the impact Maggie's actions will have on others, and her fears that she has 'rent the ties' which have given her life moral meaning (p. 597). Image patterns involving the river and water and biblical references to the Fall are prominent in this chapter, suggesting increasing conflict of duty and desire in Maggie. Her repeated statement that she would rather die than fall into this temptation suggests that her solution to her dilemma is a self-punishing one of the death of her passions or of her literal death.

BOOK SEVENTH: THE FINAL RESCUE

CHAPTER 1   **Maggie returns to the Mill and is disowned by Tom. She goes to live with the Jakins**

Five days later, Maggie fearfully returns to Dorlcote Mill. She looks exhausted and distraught, but in his bitterness that Maggie's disgraceful behaviour has frustrated his efforts to gain respectability, Tom cruelly disowns her. He informs her of Lucy's illness, indignantly rejects her explanation, and asserts his moral superiority. He goes against the spirit of the promise made to his father to 'be good' to Maggie; he will give her money, but not a home. Surprisingly, Mrs Tulliver goes with Maggie to Bob Jakin's house, where they are readily taken in. Bob shows Maggie his child, whom he has named after her, and he also expresses his affection for her with his offer to 'leather' anyone who has caused Maggie grief (p. 618). Maggie is desperate to speak to Dr Kenn, but Bob informs her that he is grieving over the recent death of his wife.

Tom is now 'master' of the Mill and asserts his full power over Maggie as older brother and as self-righteous moralist. In contrast to Maggie's wishful dream in the boat, Tom *is* angry and in returning to him, she seems partly to seek his severe judgement. Again he is contrasted with Bob, who does not blame Maggie. He does wonder, though not judgementally, how Stephen could have left her – his own action would have been far different. He readily takes her in, offers her brotherly protection and his best companion for comfort.

CHAPTER 2   **Maggie is judged by St Ogg's. She is advised and helped by Dr Kenn**

The imagined reaction of the people of St Ogg's to Maggie and Stephen's marriage, 'quite romantic!', regardless of the pain caused to Lucy and Philip, is in great contrast to the harsh view of Maggie when she returns unmarried. Despite Stephen's letter of explanation asserting Maggie's innocence, public opinion judges him to be blameless and condemns her as 'a designing bold girl' (p. 621). Tom's rejection of her only confirms their judgement. Although preoccupied with her painful feelings of remorse and love, as she walks to the rectory Maggie does become aware of how she is judged. She confesses the whole story to Dr Kenn and he understands her dilemma, but warns her that the shallow and unjust moralisers of St Ogg's will not. He tells her of Stephen's letter and advises her to leave St Ogg's. Maggie declares 'I will not go away because people say false things of me' and Dr Kenn promises to try to help her.

The narrow-mindedness and shallow inconsistency of the moral code in St Ogg's are seen at their most blatant here and the reader is made aware of how difficult Maggie's position is. The repetition of the description of the 'refined' and 'fine instinct' of public opinion implies a great contrast with Maggie's more passionate and individual instincts (pp. 620–1). This 'refinement' and moral responsibility, however, is unchristian in Dr Kenn's eyes because of the 'relaxation of ties' between the members of the community and the shallow adherence to Christian teaching (p. 625). By contrast, he interprets Maggie's motivations for returning as morally superior and thus guides the reader's interpretation.

Here again George Eliot's web metaphor is used to stress the importance of bonds between people and the increased understanding and tolerance that will ensue from recognition of those bonds. 'The great problem of the shifting relation between passion and duty' (p. 627) has always been Maggie's problem, and it is a complex one not easily solved by the application of a general moral code or reductive maxims. The tone of the final paragraph is solemn and stresses the importance of its content and message. It is in strong contrast to the light, gossipy tone of the first paragraph which mirrors its simplistic, though more conventional, methods of judging behaviour.

schismatics Protestants who are not part of the established Church of England

CHAPTER 3   **Aunt Glegg offers Maggie a home and protection and criticises Tom. Maggie receives a letter from Philip**

Surprisingly, Aunt Glegg takes Maggie's side and reproaches Tom for his rejection of her without proof. She also quarrels with Mr Glegg, whose sympathies are with Lucy. Whereas Mrs Tulliver does not know how to act in this new situation and Mrs Pullet feels too ashamed to visit St Ogg's, Mrs Glegg (made more confident by news of Stephen's letter) rises to the challenge of defending her kin against lies. Although she offers Maggie a home and protection from accusations, Maggie cannot face her Aunt's 'advice' and maintains her desire for independence. In a rare tender moment Mrs Tulliver expresses her devotion to her children. Maggie becomes increasingly anxious about Philip. He writes assuring her of his continuing loyalty and love and she is filled with painful remorse.

In the different responses of Aunt Glegg and Tom we see that the 'fundamental ideas of clanship' (p. 629), so central to the Dodson tradition, have been altered in the younger generation by 'a doubly deep dye of personal pride' (p. 631). We are encouraged to be highly critical of Tom, especially when an aunt who has always been the epitome of severity and injustice towards Maggie treats her better than he does. Our negative reaction to Tom is modified, however, by the narrator's explanation that 'like every one of us, [he] was imprisoned within the limits of his own nature' (p. 630), and also that his bitterness is so great because (unlike Aunt Glegg) he loved Maggie when they were children. The reference to their childhood as 'the time when they had clasped tiny fingers together' (p. 630) recalls Maggie's first memory and helps to prepare us for their final union when Tom's hatred and pride will not divide them. Philip's letter reveals his nobleness and his insight into Maggie's character. The harmony between them is suggested by his words, which touch on the visual as well as musical images used to signal Maggie's passionate nature.

CHAPTER 4   **Dr Kenn offers Maggie work as a governess to his children. Lucy visits Maggie secretly**

Dr Kenn fails to change the minds of his female parishioners about Maggie and so offers her work with his own younger children to demonstrate that she is not a moral danger. This immediately leads to malicious gossip about the relationship between Maggie and Dr Kenn. Fearing that Maggie does still want to marry Stephen and aiming to ensure that Stephen should return to Lucy, the Miss Guests propose to take Lucy with them to Scarborough, planning that Stephen should join them there. Maggie is eager for news of Lucy and longs to see her. Just before her departure, Lucy secretly visits Maggie to tell her she is forgiven and to express her love, sympathy and admiration for Maggie. She promises to visit again when she returns from Scarborough.

> The narrow-minded community of St Ogg's is severely criticised: the women for their self-serving prejudice against Maggie, and the men for their secret love of scandal, their jokes at Maggie's expense and their failure to counter the malice of the women. The minority who do have sympathy with Maggie are too timid to stand up to the majority. As readers, we are also implicated in the prejudice of these reactions and made to question our own intolerances. Lucy's affection and admiration for Maggie not only

contrast with the doubts and suspicions of the Miss Guests, but also raise her in our estimation – she recognises that Maggie is 'better' than her in having greater moral strength and determination (p. 643). Rejecting the literary convention of the divisive dichotomy of dark and fair heroines, George Eliot unites her two very different heroines in a loving sisterhood. Maggie's brooding on the 'flowing river', however, bodes ill.

Peter's denial Peter denied Christ three times and wept bitterly afterwards

CHAPTER 5   **The Floss floods and Maggie attempts to rescue Tom. Both drown but are finally united in death**

The day after Lucy's visit the weather suddenly changes, prompting the older inhabitants of St Ogg's to recall the great floods of sixty years previously. Awake during a stormy night, Maggie is newly desolate because Dr Kenn, warned about the damaging effects of the gossip, has ended her employment and advised her again to leave St Ogg's. She has also received a letter from Stephen which begs her to end his misery by calling him to her. Although tempted and, in the face of his despair, having doubts about her decision, Maggie's recollection of Lucy's presence and Philip's letter lead her to burn Stephen's letter and finally to renounce him. As she prays for strength to bear the lifelong pain of her resolution, she becomes aware that the house is flooding. She wakes Bob, and they manage to get into two boats, but Maggie is swept away, adrift on the floodwater. At first Maggie feels only that this is an escape from a life she had dreaded, but with the first light she courageously heads towards the Mill to try to rescue Tom and her mother. She saves Tom and they aim to rescue Lucy, but their boat is struck by wooden machinery. Tom clasps Maggie and they drown embracing each other.

> Ironically, it is Dr Kenn's role as clergyman that eventually forces him to bow down to public pressure and to go against his own conscience and sense of what is morally right. In contrast with Philip's letter, Stephen's reveals him to be largely self-concerned. As her self-questioning suggests, Maggie longs for death because it seems to be the only way to escape from temptation. Although this ending has been anticipated by hints and forebodings throughout

the novel, it does seem uncharacteristically melodramatic and abrupt, and the reversion to an idealised relationship between Tom and Maggie (we have never seen such harmony between them as the last line of the chapter suggests) seems unlikely, even in such desperate circumstances. Indeed, Tom's sudden realisation of his sister's immense courage and strength, and his recognition of her moral goodness and her innocence which fill him with 'awe and humiliation' (p. 654) seem to fulfil much of what Maggie has wished for throughout.

Death is Maggie's escape from what she perceives as 'her real temptation' (p. 647) and her being swept away seems like a dream. That 'the threads of ordinary association were broken' (p. 651), suggests that the social threads that have bound her to others and which have driven her action throughout are also broken, seemingly defeating the object of her struggle. Despite the break with realism, this final event does make sense in terms of the symbolic and metaphorical dimensions of the novel. That Tom gains insight into 'the depths in life' (p. 654) seems a particularly apt metaphor for signalling his recognition of meaning and feeling beyond the limitations of conventional and rational understanding.

CONCLUSION

After five years there is little trace of the damage caused by the flood and only Tom and Maggie have died. However, the landscape and the hearts of those who loved Tom and Maggie are irrevocably scarred by the past 'ravages' of nature (p. 656). We discover that Stephen and Philip have been visiting the tomb where Maggie and Tom are buried, although there is no mention of Mrs Tulliver. Philip is always solitary, but Stephen is later accompanied by Lucy, suggesting that they are married.

The conclusion is very brief and impersonal, and we are placed at a distance from characters in whose lives we have been intimately involved. The intensity of the contradictory feelings, 'keenest joy and keenest sorrow', of Stephen and Philip provides a sense of harmony in grief, and Tom and Maggie's epitaph from the biblical lament of David for Saul and Jonathan has likewise been read as suggesting permanent reconciliation in death. However, Kristen Brady argues that this is not the case (*George Eliot*, Macmillan, 1992). She suggests that the epitaph actually excludes Maggie, since the biblical story it refers to is concerned only with male rivalry and male bonding. She argues that Maggie's desires are not met in this ending, but continue to be denied.

'In their death they were not divided' from David's lament for Saul and Jonathan, 2 Samuel 1:23

PART THREE

CRITICAL APPROACHES

CHARACTERISATION

George Eliot's characters are created not only with a sense of their external characteristics (physical appearance, social and economic status), but importantly, also with a strongly developed psychological dimension. She shows us the inner workings of her characters' minds and we see the complex motivations for their actions and behaviour. We see the ways that they reason and make sense of their own actions, and how memory and experience contribute to the formation of character. As one critic states 'Her imagination … is an X-ray, bringing them [her characters] to life by the clearness with which she penetrates to the secret mainspring of their actions' (David Cecil, in G.S. Haight, ed., *A Century of George Eliot Criticism*, Methuen, 1965, p. 201).

This psychological insight is a crucial factor in George Eliot's wider purpose of increasing her readers' tolerance of difference and insisting that we should understand each other better. As she stated in a letter to Charles Bray: 'If Art does not enlarge men's sympathies, it does nothing morally … the only effect I ardently long to produce by my writings, is that those who read them should be better able to *imagine* and to *feel* the pains and the joys of those who differ from themselves in everything but the broad fact of being struggling erring human creatures' (in John Cross, *George Eliot's Life, as Related in her Letters and Journals*, William Blackwood and Sons, 1885, p. 279). Her narrative comments largely guide the reader away from harsh judgements and we are encouraged to feel sympathy for her characters, however mistaken their actions seem to be.

George Eliot humanises her characters in the sense that they are morally mixed and cannot be defined as wholly good or bad. Later Victorian writers mocked what they saw as a simplistic depiction of character in earlier moralistic writing; this is summed up in Oscar Wilde's quip that 'The good ended happily, and the bad unhappily. That is what fiction means' (*The Importance of Being Earnest* (1895), Methuen, 1966, p. 28). However, George Eliot's characters defy such reductive categorisation. Many exhibit a complex sense of morality which makes it hard to absolutely condone or reject the decisions they make. In *The Mill on the Floss*, George Eliot's characters seem to fall into oppositions (Maggie and Tom, Philip and Stephen, Maggie and Lucy), but her main characters are shown to be contradictory and are open to several interpretations.

  Although innate characteristics are crucial for the development of George Eliot's characters, she does not simply suggest that 'character is destiny'. For instance, her speculation about the fate of Hamlet suggests that had he not been subject to the actions of others he may have had a quite different destiny (p. 514). Family and society, as well as chance and bad luck, then, have a profound effect on destiny and character development. She emphasises the bonds between characters, the constrictions of social conventions, and the connection with the past as factors that influence her characters' decisions and prevent them from being free agents. This illustrates her belief in the interactive and organic nature of society (see Historical Background – Thought and Belief). She uses 'web' imagery to express these constraints on her characters, especially in *The Mill on the Floss* and *Middlemarch*. However, she also suggests that it is only by working within this web that there can be a steady social change or evolution. In the absence of faith in a monotheistic Christian God, George Eliot was trying to form a moral framework from the past in which a sense of duty is paramount.

  In *The Mill on the Floss*, we see how character traits are modified or compounded by experience and environment. In *Critical Essays on George Eliot* (1970) Barbara Hardy suggests that George Eliot's characters are 'stubborn and unchanging' and although they may act 'out of character' in response to 'strong external pressures', that this is only a temporary transformation (Hardy, ed., Routledge and Kegan Paul, p. 56). A later critic, Sally Shuttleworth, sees the cultural environment as having a more profound impact. She discusses George Eliot's development of character in terms of socially constructed gender identities: 'Eliot is not merely depicting the troubles faced by a Victorian woman, but exploring how social conflicts are inscribed within the self, and how identity, both male and female, is created by the internalization of proffered subject positions' ('Critical Commentary' of the Routledge edition of *The Mill on the Floss*, 1991, p. 497). This suggests that character development is affected by the expectations placed on male and female characters, and the differing opportunities available to them.

MAGGIE TULLIVER

Early critics judged Maggie's characterisation as inconsistent: 'the young woman with the overmastering passion is very slightly connected to the Maggie of the Mill' (in David Carroll, *George Eliot: the Critical Heritage*, Routledge and Kegan Paul, 1971, p. 119). Later critics consider Maggie's relationship with Stephen as 'consistent' and 'credibly developed' (David Cecil, in Haight, *A Century of George Eliot Criticism*, p. 200). Others see her as an autobiographical self: F.R. Leavis is one of many who assumes that 'Maggie Tulliver is essentially identical with young Mary Ann Evans' (in Haight, p. 240).

Maggie is a complex and somewhat contradictory character and she has prompted several different responses and interpretations. She is both a **Romantic** character (intuitive, imaginative, passionate, idealistic) and a dutiful daughter and sister (devoted, tender and longing to give and receive love). Her impetuous and violent behaviour has been likened to that of her father (stressing the theme of heredity, and her anomalous identity as a woman with masculine character traits), and her anger seen as a symbol of feminist frustration and rage at the oppression of women in Victorian society. As a child, Maggie is dreamy and forgetful, as well as astute, clever and proud of her intelligence. She is reckless and impetuous, 'naughty' her mother claims, but also masochistic and readily takes on blame and guilt. As a child and an adult, her desperate longing for admiration and love is a central aspect of her character. She is in many ways psychologically real, and she struggles to bring the conflicting aspects of her identity into harmony, as we see in her relationships with men.

Her family environment is central to her problematic sense of her identity as a woman. For instance, although her father praises Maggie's intelligence and quickness, he also maintains the socially conventional view that 'an over 'cute woman's no better nor a long-tailed sheep' (p. 60). Similarly, his reasons for choosing Bessy for his wife reinforce this sexist prejudice. Her mother and her aunts constantly bemoan Maggie's lack of femininity, comparing her unfavourably with the epitome of the feminine ideal, Lucy Deane. In her constant favouring of Tom, Mrs Tulliver repeatedly asserts Maggie's inferior status. Tom asserts his superiority as a male and although they have a similar view of the future (with Maggie as housekeeper to Tom), his assumption of the role of protector with the power to 'punish her when she did wrong' (p. 92) differs wildly from hers, where she will assume a conventionally male role as source of wisdom (p. 81).

Maggie rejects the conventional definition of femininity in many ways, but her experience repeatedly defeats her striving for equality. She clashes with the world of St Ogg's in almost every way, but this environment enforces conventional gender ideals and encourages Maggie's sense of duty and submission. Her contradictory unruliness and vulnerability can be seen as signs of the disjunction between her individual needs and the social demands and values placed on her as a woman. The narrator's and author's sympathy for Maggie, however, keep the reader firmly on her side – 'poor Maggie' and 'poor child' are phrases repeatedly inviting our sympathy.

Like Dorothea Brooke in *Middlemarch*, Maggie is searching for a system of belief that would offer moral guidance, but finds there is no easy answer to the dilemma of conscience and desire. Maggie, again like Dorothea, aspires to acquire 'masculine' knowledge. However, books are not only a source of information and learning for Maggie (as her Latin lesson to Tom demonstrates). They also fire her imagination and give the reader insight into her inner life; they foster her dreamy and imaginative nature and provide an escape from her constraining present.

TOM TULLIVER

In many ways Tom is Maggie's opposite and as with Maggie we see how his childhood character traits develop as he matures. He has inherited his mother's features and Dodson characteristics, he is narrow-minded and adheres rigidly and unquestioningly to conventional values and gender stereotypes. However, he is also very much like his father in his inflexibility and his aggressive response to anything that may challenge his superior masculine position. He has not inherited his father's more positive traits, such as generosity, and although he promises his father that he will care for 'the little wench'(p. 463), he interprets this not in the warm and loving way his father intended, but coldly in terms of financial provision and discipline.

As a child and adult, Tom never doubts himself and is self-righteous in his moral judgements. As a child he assumed superiority over Maggie because of his privileged social position as a boy; as an adult this sense of male superiority is endorsed by dominant cultural assumptions. With the exception of his education, the opportunities Tom is given are conducive to his character traits. The necessary focus on work and his progress in the economic sphere accord with his single-minded attitude and his natural abilities. He considers that his experience of the public world gives him the power to dictate Maggie's actions and to demand her obedience: 'a brother, who goes out into the world and mixes with men, necessarily knows better what is right and respectable for his sister than she can know herself' (p. 504). However, he lacks imagination and is intellectually limited. As an adult his arrogance and blindness to his own faults and his inability to see the complexity of relationships and moral decisions means that he is a cold and compassionless defender of what are revealed as inadequate dominant social values. In *George Eliot (Marian Evans) A Literary Life*, Kerry McSweeney calls him 'the novel's dominant symbol of repressive male authority' (Macmillan, 1991, p. 92).

In George Eliot's depiction of Tom we see both her endorsement and criticism of Victorian gender identities. At times the author seems to approve of an innate manliness in Tom (for example in his protective feelings towards Laura Stelling he displays 'the fibre that turns to true manliness', p. 213), but she also sees masculinity as inadequate and negative, bound up as it is in Tom's case with prejudice, bitterness and resentment. It is 'manly feeling', and the accompanying 'strength of will, conscious rectitude of purpose, narrowness of imagination and intellect, great power of self-control and a disposition to exert control over others', that are criticised when Lucy tries to persuade Tom to accept Maggie's relationship with Philip (p. 579).

George Eliot did not perceive Tom negatively, however, and in answer to E.S. Dallas's harsh criticism stated that she 'painted [Tom] with respect' (in David Carroll, *George Eliot: the Critical Heritage*, Routledge and Kegan Paul, 1971, p. 162). He is hard-working and, in the financial crisis that ensues after his father's lawsuit, he acts in an admirable way. We, like Maggie, must admire his determination.

Further, the author uses narrative comment to encourage the reader to sympathise with Tom. At the point at which our hostility for him may be greatest, as he disowns Maggie in her time of greatest need, the narrative voice draws the reader into the situation by asserting our common human failings: 'Tom, like every one of us, was imprisoned within the limits of his own nature' (p. 630). The mention of his memory of the intensity of his bond with Maggie as a child seems strategically placed to win our sympathy here, especially as the words echo Maggie's memory of this source of sibling love. There is some debate about what Tom discovers about Maggie in the moment before they both drown, but it is possible to say that Tom does realise not only that he has misjudged Maggie, but also that he has repressed and denied a large part of himself. This opens the way for a more positive interpretation of this character.

STEPHEN GUEST

Generally, critics consider George Eliot's creation of Stephen, and Maggie's desire for him, to be a great flaw in the novel. In F.R. Leavis's estimation Stephen is 'universally accepted to be a sad lapse on George Eliot's part', 'unmistakably feminine', 'a provincial dandy', and Maggie's love for him is 'incredible and insufferable' (in Haight, p. 241). Earlier criticism produced a much more violent reaction, however. Algernon Charles Swinburne summed up Stephen as 'a cur so far beneath the chance of promotion to the notice of [any man's] horsewhip, or elevation to the level of his boot', and another review referred to his 'dishonourable abduction of Maggie' (in Haight, p. 127, and Carroll, p. 141). Much nineteenth- and twentieth-century criticism of Stephen is disapproving; he is condemned for being insensitive, egotistical, selfish, dishonourable, contemptuous and manipulative. George Eliot makes use of narrative intrusion in order to maintain sympathy for him, although she also adopts an **ironic** tone that mocks his pretensions and vanity.

Stephen is a conventional representative of a middle-class provincial society. His reasons for choosing Lucy to be his wife demonstrate this:

> Was not Stephen Guest right in his decided opinion that this slim maiden of eighteen was quite the sort of wife a man would not be likely to repent of

marrying? [...] A man likes his wife to be pretty: well, Lucy was pretty, but not to a maddening extent. A man likes his wife to be accomplished, gentle, affectionate and not stupid; and Lucy had all these qualifications [...] she was a little darling, and exactly the sort of woman he had always most admired. (pp. 477–8)

His attitude towards women is condescending, and like Mr Tulliver he wants a wife he can dominate. However, he lacks any real understanding of Lucy and fails to perceive her 'rarest quality' (p. 477). He is handsome, charming, educated, but also vain and possessive. Part of what attracts him to Maggie is the challenge of possessing and dominating a woman like her, significantly she is reduced to a 'creature': 'To see such a creature subdued by love for one would be a lot worth having – to another man' (p. 523). The disclaimer added to this thought is not convincing here and invites criticism of the evasiveness and dishonesty of his character.

Having said this, he is on the whole more honest about his feelings for Maggie than she is about her feelings for him (as Haight suggests, p. 345). His affection and passion for Maggie is genuine. He may be 'a provincial dandy', given his 'diamond ring, attar of roses, and air of nonchalant leisure at twelve o'clock in the day' (p. 469), but he is not a rake, as the comparison with the woman-hunting Torry makes clear. His singing allures Maggie and he in turn is enthralled by her magnificent beauty and unconventionality (see Critical Approaches – Patterns of Imagery, Metaphors, Symbols). The magnetic attraction between them draws Stephen out of his conventional mindset and, against his better judgement, he is attracted to the 'devil' in Maggie, and to her contradictory character as revealed in her eyes.

The introduction given to Stephen Guest in the novel creates immediate doubts about him: his leisure is the result of the labour of others and he cruelly snips the scissors at Minny, the dog given as a gift by Tom (it has been suggested that this cruelty is an expression of rivalry with Tom for Lucy's affections). In comparison with Maggie's self-sacrifice and Philip's eventual altruism (as his final letter shows), Stephen seems to act selfishly. However, although his final letter is partly an aspect of his emotional manipulation of Maggie, he does suffer and the hurt he expresses in this letter is genuine. In many ways the pressure he tries to put on Maggie is more acceptable than the pressures Philip exerts, because we know that Stephen's desire and love for Maggie is reciprocated. However, we also know that he does not and cannot understand the more complex and deeply felt dilemma that she is experiencing.

PHILIP WAKEM

Sensitive, intelligent, talented, artistic, gentle and kind, Philip seems to be an ideal match for certain aspects of Maggie's character. However, the result of his childhood accident has not only emasculated him physically, but has feminised his behaviour as well and he holds no sexual attraction for her. He is repeatedly contrasted with Stephen and his appearance and behaviour are often associated with femininity: as a child his hair 'waved and curled at the ends like a girl's' (p. 234), and as an adult he has nerves 'as sensitive as a woman's' (p. 543). He is acutely sensitive to the response of others and his pride leads him to feel bitter and resentful when he feels he is being pitied. His pride in his intelligence also leads to a superior attitude towards Tom when Tom first arrives at Mr Stelling's house, although this is modified by his own experience of the pain of humiliation:

> Philip felt some bitter complacency in the promising stupidity of this well-made active-looking boy; but made polite by his own extreme sensitiveness as well as by his desire to conciliate, he checked his inclination to laugh (p. 235)

Philip is in many ways a noble character and, like Maggie, is prepared to make sacrifices for the happiness of others, as his final letter to Maggie amply demonstrates. His sensitivity also means that he is perceptive and makes illuminating comments which help our understanding of many characters, Maggie and Tom, for instance. However, he is not entirely virtuous – he feels the pangs of jealousy and is very temperamental. He also manipulates Maggie's feelings, even though he knows that Maggie sees him only as a brother figure, a teacher and friend. Like Stephen, he puts his desires first and through emotional appeals tries to pressure her into making a commitment to him (Book 5, Chapter 4). Tom's discovery and ending of the relationship between Maggie and Philip disgusts Maggie, although she also feels some relief that it is over. Critics have argued that at this point Tom acts as a **character double** for Maggie, acting out her deepest wishes which she can not openly articulate.

Philip also manipulates his father in a similar way. He plays on his father's pity and on his attachment to his now dead wife in order to secure his father's support in trying to marry Maggie. Like Stephen, he perceives Maggie to be an object that he wants to possess. Not only has he objectified her twice in his paintings of her, but part of his appeal to his father is that his father has the power to deprive him of 'the only *thing* that would make my life worth having' (p. 542, my emphasis). Although Philip seems to be unlike his father in very many ways, it is worth pointing out that it is Mr Wakem who has the most derogatory words to say about women in the novel: 'We don't ask what a woman does – we ask whom she belongs to' (pp. 542–3). However, throughout the novel, authorial intervention maintains our sympathy for Philip, and we are instructed 'not [to] think too hardly of Philip' (p. 430).

LUCY DEANE

Lucy is in many ways the angelic opposite of Maggie. In Victorian ideology and iconography women were dichotomously defined as either angelic (pure, passive and ideally feminine) or demonic (subversive or defiant in some way of feminine ideals, and 'fallen' sexually). In literature too this opposition prevailed in that the fair and good woman was always rewarded (usually with marriage to the hero). Many women writers mocked such facile and limited depictions of women, especially those found in the popular sensationalist fiction written in the second half of the century. George Eliot also explicitly mocks this dichotomy and its moral message for women as Maggie criticises the depiction of dark and fair heroines in the books Philip lends to her and demands that the balance be restored: 'If you could give me some story, now, where the dark woman triumphs, it would restore the balance' (p. 433). Philip's teasing remark that Maggie would steal her fair cousin's lover is in fact prophetic, but George Eliot seems to be disclaiming a simplistic interpretation of this in terms of the actions and consequent rewards for good and bad heroines.

Lucy is angelic – 'aerial' is a word often used to describe her. She is 'little pink-and-white Lucy' (p. 164), and as a child is perfectly feminine, quiet, obedient, and passive. As a woman she is self-effacing, charming and kind to small creatures. In her reference to Maggie's ability to be beautiful without the feminine accoutrements of fine clothes and to her knowledge as 'witchery' (p. 480), and to her intelligence as 'uncanniness' (p. 498), Lucy seems to endorse conventional views of women who do not conform to Victorian gender ideals. However, she is a more complex character than this would lead us to believe and, as her active reassurance of Maggie at the end of the novel shows, she has the capacity for deep feeling, as well as integrity and commitment.

MR TULLIVER

Headstrong, rash, irritable, prejudiced, incompetent, obsessed with control, proud, ill-informed, vindictive and inflexible have been some of the criticisms levelled at Mr Tulliver. His sexist treatment of his wife and rigid adherence to the **patriarchal** value system, his irrational risks and financial errors, in conjunction with his own assessment of himself as a good husband and as a man of substance, all contribute to a lack of sympathy for this character. His pride that Dorlcote Mill has been in his family for generations is incompatible with his wanting to educate Tom so that he will not be a rival to him or inherit the Mill. His plans for his son are compatible, however, with his need to exert control at home, over his wife and children, and in his business, over the river and over other rivals.

Despite his limitations, Mr Tulliver's genuine love for his daughter and sister, his warmth and generosity redeem him as a character. His lack of respect for his wife, though not presented positively, is balanced by her apparent lack of concern for his ill-health and her obsessive focus on her possessions. Further, we have sympathy for him when we realise that his impetuous behaviour is in part a result of his inability to adapt to change as rapidly as is necessary. His struggles to understand the legal system leave him feeling vulnerable and confused, and George Eliot's negative and cynical depiction of this legal system in the form of Wakem put us on Mr Tulliver's side. His illness generates great sympathy for him, as does his admirable concern for and generosity to his sister, and his honourable wish to repay his debts. Although his pagan vengeance and eventual attack against Wakem are disturbing, his final demise is moving.

MRS TULLIVER

From the very beginning of the text we see that Mrs Tulliver is materialistic and takes obvious pleasure in the possessions she has, not for the enjoyment they afford her in their use, but for the effect they will produce on others when she is dead. Like her sisters she has no sense of a spiritual afterlife but is concerned purely with public opinion and her reputation. She is in no way a match for her husband in terms of intellect or assertiveness. Her only independent action in going to Mr Wakem leads to further trouble. However, as silly as she is in many respects, she is not wholly without redeeming features. Critics have generally noted George Eliot's depiction of inadequate mother figures in her novels, and refer to Mrs Tulliver and Mrs Stelling in *The Mill on the Floss* as examples. Mrs Tulliver *is* largely critical of her naughty daughter, only showing her kindness when Maggie conforms to feminine norms, but she does defend Maggie against the harsh **patriarchal** judgements that Tom, and St Ogg's society generally, make about her. She also appears to make an astute comment about the superficiality of those with authority and education: 'them fine-talking men from the big towns mostly wear the false shirt-fronts; they wear a frill till it's all a mess, and then hide it with a bib' (p. 59). Probably, she herself misses the significance of her words, but through them George Eliot prepares the reader for the fact that neither Riley nor Mr Stelling are quite what they seem.

THE DODSONS

Early reception of the Dodson sisters was not positive, 'stingy, selfish wretches' was E.S. Dallas's interpretation (in Carroll, p. 135). G.S. Haight's later assessment is not much better: 'Conventional, conservative, unimaginative, they make the accumulation of property their principle concern in life' (in Haight, p. 340). George Eliot herself responded to the negative assessments of the Dodsons with surprise and defended their religion of respectability as one followed by the majority of English people. They are not explored psychologically as the main characters are, however, and as F.R. Leavis suggests they are of 'sociological interest' in the novel (in Haight, p. 140). They are representatives of a narrow-minded, prejudiced and self-centred provincial middle-class community for whom family ties are central but not affectionate. Their main preoccupation is death and what they see as the accompanying opportunity to prove their superiority in terms of their principled provision of inheritance, and the general order and high level of respectability with which their lives are conducted.

We are given a clear sense of them as individuals and collectively they represent the stifling social constraints on Maggie. Their authority is undermined, and the severity softened, however, by the comedy with which they are represented. Their unquestioning sense of superiority is challenged by the fact that the Miss Guests consider them to be 'vulgar'. Although their sense of kinship may be harsh, at the time of real necessity both Mrs Glegg and Mrs Tulliver defend and try to protect Maggie.

BOB JAKIN

Bob is a minor character, though what he represents is important. As one critic suggests 'Jakin's friendly support for his Tulliver friends is more than sentimentality; it is part of a general philosophy of observing the signs, recovering from adversity, insuring against loss, profiting from unexpected windfalls, which humanity needs if it is to progress' (A. W. Bellringer, in *George Eliot*, Macmillan, 1993, p. 60). Uneducated, Bob makes his way in the world by taking advantage of the opportunities that come his way, and turning negatives into positives. He acts as a contrast not only to Tom, but also to the Dodson approach to finances. He is kind and generous in wanting to share his good fortune, and provides shelter to Tom and Maggie at crucial times. Because of the class difference he has little chance of a romantic relationship with Maggie. As a potential lover he is chivalrous and affectionate and acts as a contrast to both Philip and Stephen: unlike them he does not manipulate or pressure Maggie; he simply demonstrates his admiration for her, acts kindly, and offers to defend her honour by 'leather[ing]' her enemies (p. 618).

THE NARRATOR

One of the most striking features of the opening of *The Mill on the Floss* is the way that the reader is drawn into the world of the novel by the colloquial tone used by the narrator as he casually begins to tell the story. According to Janice Carlisle in *The Sense of an Audience: Dickens, Thackeray, and George Eliot at Mid-Century* (The Harvester Press, 1982), the characteristic use of a self-conscious narrator as a mediating presence between the reader, the text and the author was one means by which Victorian novelists fulfilled what they saw as their moral responsibility as writers. Since the moral implications and intentions of the mid-nineteenth-century novel were more important than at any other time, it was crucial that this moral purpose be fulfilled as effectively as possible. Techniques, such as the use of an **omniscient narrator**, direct address to the reader, and the use of present-tense narration all aim to encourage reader involvement in the novel and to increase the reader's sympathy for the characters and their lives. In *The Mill on the Floss*, the use of an omniscient narrator, who intervenes with analytical comments and statements of opinion about how to interpret events and character, and about human life and experience in general, serves to guide the reader's judgement and to determine the reader's response to the characters and the events. Although George Eliot mostly uses this narrator to analyse and give opinions, occasionally the intervening voice seems to be that of the author herself, thus offering another point of view expressed through authorial intervention.

Some critics discuss the narrative voice in *The Mill on the Floss* as being female, seeing it simply as George Eliot speaking; others argue that the narrative voice is androgynous. However, internal textual evidence marks it clearly as male; for example, the voice assumes a masculine authority and invites comparison with male experience (p. 250). Discussion of the narrator has also focused on whether he is a member of the community of St Ogg's or a detached outsider. Michael Wheeler, in *English Fiction of the Victorian Period 1830–1890* (Longman, 1985), sums him up as 'a thinker: meditative, moral and philosophical', and Kerry McSweeney suggests that he 'resembles a social scientist observing the effects of hereditary conditions on an organism' (Wheeler, p. 120, McSweeney, p. 90). His attitude to the characters is sometimes critical or mocking, but always sympathetic, especially towards Maggie, with whom he is identified at the beginning of the novel as he dreams about seeing her by the Mill.

The crucial thing about the creation of the narrator, as far as fulfilling the moral purpose of the novel goes, is that the reader trusts him enough to agree with his opinion and accept his moral guidance. George Eliot builds our trust in her narrator by the many examples of the balanced and reasoned assessments of character and situations and the psychological insight he offers. Through his appeals to the reader's judgement and his use of the direct address 'you' and the collusive 'we' and 'our', we are led to agree with his criticisms of mistaken attitudes and hypocritical, ignorant and arrogantly self-righteous assumptions. A good example of this narrative technique is seen in the discussion of the opinion held by the people of St Ogg's regarding Maggie's return after eloping with Stephen. Here, the narrator mocks public opinion and invites the reader to collude with his opinion with the use of 'we know' (p. 620).

At times the assumptions made about the reader's taste, education, class, status and gender may alienate the modern reader a little, as might the assumption that we will share the narrator's attachment to the past and to the place with which he is so familiar. His assumption of a superior moral understanding and the capacity to speak the truth unproblematically, known as the **hierarchy of discourses** in **classic realist texts**, has also been criticised for its didacticism. However, the narrator's comments in *The Mill on the Floss* also serve to ensure that details are not missed: 'Had anything remarkable happened?' is asked after Maggie has met Stephen, and we are told why it was remarkable (p. 494). We are also alerted to aspects of character which may not be apparent to the characters themselves, for instance, the fact that Maggie does not realise the extent of her emotional attachments when she confesses to Lucy (p. 498).

OTHER TECHNIQUES

The use of present-tense narration is a narrative convention found in many Victorian novels. George Eliot uses it to engage the reader's attention by creating a sense of immediacy and direct involvement with events and characters. She also uses **rhetorical questions** to engage the reader's opinion, as well as **allusion** to other texts that her readers would almost certainly have read, such as William Wordsworth's *The Prelude*, John Milton's *Paradise Lost* and John Bunyan's *The Pilgrim's Progress*. This would not only involve the reader in the novel by drawing on something familiar, but also extend the moral meaning of George Eliot's text.

REALISM

George Eliot's employment of the narrative convention of **realism** is another means by which she sought to establish a connection with the reader in order to make effective the moral intention of her writing. According to Michael Wheeler, Victorian writers used the convention of realism 'to engage directly and consistently with the complexities of human experience in the real world' (p. 7). By presenting a fictional world which resembles the real world, realism stresses the sincerity of representation and hence hopes to engage the reader's sympathies. In her essay 'The Natural History of German Life', George Eliot argues: 'Art is the nearest thing to life; it is a mode of amplifying experience and extending our contact with our fellow-men beyond the bounds of our personal lot. All the more sacred is the task of the artist when he undertakes to paint the life of the People' (in Thomas Pinney, *Essays of George Eliot*, Routledge and Kegan Paul, 1963, p. 270).

George Eliot aims to construct a narrative which is realistic in terms of setting, situation, dialogue, manners, and idiom, and also one in which characters exhibit psychological and emotional realism as well. Following William Wordsworth, she saw realism as depicting the ordinary life of social classes not usually depicted in literature (or else treated with ridicule). In *The Mill on the Floss* she focused on the provincial middle-classes, depicting the realistic detail of their everyday lives. Like Sir Walter Scott, George Eliot is concerned with the moral decisions individuals make in a complex society (as Wheeler suggests, p. 8).

However, George Eliot also resisted a simplistic equation between life and fiction. She did not see the realistic mode she employed as mimetic (a theory of representation which aims to create a mirror reflection of life). Her narrator in *Adam Bede*, for instance, aims at a faithful representation of life, but admits that it can never be purely this, given that it is mediated through the narrator's mind (and actually stems from the author's imagination). The mirror he holds up to life, then, offers only a 'defective', 'disturbed', 'faint' and 'confused' reflection (*Adam Bede*, Penguin, p. 221).

George Eliot breaks with **realism** in *The Mill on the Floss* when neither Maggie nor Tom speak in the dialect used by their parents. She also appeals to a **Romantic** bond with nature, privileges the transcendent power of imagination and sensuality, and draws on mythic elements. The ending of the novel has caused many critics difficulties for several reasons, and the flood is central to early criticisms of George Eliot's break with realism. Henry James, F. R. Leavis and Barbara Hardy all find the ending problematic: a 'final unsuccessful resort to solution by fantasy' (Hardy, *Critical Essays*, p. 45). Later critics perceive this break with realism in different ways: as privileging thematic coherence rather than realism, as illustrating the inadequacy of the realist mode, and as suggesting the lack of choices for Victorian women.

STYLE AND LANGUAGE

These aspects of George Eliot's writing are closely linked to narrative technique and moral purpose. She uses a variety of styles in *The Mill on the Floss*; her prose is often complex and metaphorical, although she also uses colloquialisms, humour and **irony** to great effect. The Dodson sisters with all their peculiarities and prejudices are the main sources of comedy, and irony is used to diminish social pretensions, as in the passage about 'good society' (p. 385–6). Mocking **satire** is also used to expose hypocrisy and limited moral sensibility, as in the description of public opinion about Maggie's return to St Ogg's unmarried (p. 619–21).

George Eliot's use of dialogue and analysis both contributes to her moral purpose of depicting ordinary individuals and helps generate a sympathetic response. For instance, the idioms used in Mr Tulliver's dialogue not only give rise to humour, but also help to create a sense of his no-nonsense character: 'I'll niver pull my coat off before I go to bed. [...] I shan't be put off wi' spoon-meat afore I've lost my teeth' (p. 65). George Eliot's style has been criticised for its preoccupation with analysis, but we can see that guiding the reader's response is crucial in order for the book to succeed in its moral intention. There are several instances where the author closely examines a character's motivation, making clear the difficulty of reaching a moral judgement. The detailed and extended analysis of Mr Riley's motivation for recommending Mr Stelling is the first instance of this (pp. 74–7), and Wakem's motivation in buying Dorlcote Mill another obvious example (pp. 338–41). The often complex analytical sections also force the reader to read slowly and carefully, thus increasing our engagement with the characters and their situations.

The complexity of George Eliot's style may seem excessive in places; in others it attempts to convey the workings of her characters' minds and to raise our sympathy for the predicaments the characters are in. The quite unwieldy paragraph describing Mr Tulliver's reaction to the loss of his lawsuit is apt given the state of mind he is in. In fact, like the later **stream of consciousness** technique used by twentieth-century writers, it describes what is passing through his mind, 'a rush of projects in his brain', and his thoughts flitting between plans to remedy his situation, as well as recalling other financial burdens. The style is both revealing and realistic in the circumstances (p. 273). With his constant self-reassurances we see that Mr Tulliver does not want to admit defeat, and that he is attempting to bolster his confidence in the face of disaster.

George Eliot's style is also at times pictorial. This was especially the case with *Adam Bede*, and in the opening chapter of *The Mill on the Floss* the landscape and scene at Dorlcote Mill is 'painted' for us with evocative detail. This picture illustrates three key and interconnected elements that will be developed in the novel – the relationship between human and animal, the inevitable process of industrialisation, and the importance of childhood in Maggie's life.

As well as employing dialect to create a sense of realism, and a sometimes humorous lack of communication between characters (for example, between Mr and Mrs Tulliver), George Eliot also makes use of implicit value judgements about language to influence our opinions of characters. We discover that Mr Tulliver was right not to trust the puzzling language of the law, and it seems significant that the painful metaphor used to express Wakem's enjoyment of his power over Mr Tulliver (of Mr Tulliver having his 'rough tongue filed by a sense of obligation') is one that also alludes to Wakem's sense of superiority given

Mr Tulliver's non-standard English speech (p. 340). The use of dialect also signals a social difference between characters – Bob is of a lower class than Maggie, and Mrs Tulliver of a lower class than Wakem, for instance.

George Eliot also opens up discussion of the multiple and ambiguous meanings of language. Maggie's Latin reveals that words can have more than one meaning (p. 214), and on several occasions the author points out that language conceals as well as reveals feelings (p. 437). Further, George Eliot explores the more coded ways of communicating illicit feelings: music and the longing looks that they exchange become a language expressing Maggie and Stephen's desire, their circumspect flirtation is a 'trivial language' (p. 535), and their silence in the conservatory is a 'mute confession' of their reciprocal desire (p. 561).

STRUCTURE

The Mill on the Floss has been described as a novel about growing up female in Victorian England. However, it does not follow the usual **Bildungsroman** structure, which traces the development of a central character, traditionally a boy, through several 'rite of passage' experiences. Usually, at the celebratory end of such narratives the protagonist successfully assumes his identity and vocation. Instead, George Eliot's novel has a double Bildungsroman structure which offers a contrast between male and female experiences and development.

Although not a 'scholard' and taking after his mother's side of the family, Tom achieves a considerable degree of success as he fulfils the social and familial expectations placed on him and assumes a manly and responsible role as the breadwinner of the family. Maggie's development, on the other hand, is fraught with conflict and contradiction as she struggles to express a sense of self which is contrary to social and familial expectations. Instead of experiencing a sense of wholeness, Maggie is deeply divided and does not resolve her feelings of anxiety, isolation and alienation.

The traditional linear progression of the Bildungsroman narrative structure is disrupted both because childhood incidents **foreshadow** future events, and because Maggie's past, her desires and impetuous actions, cannot be left behind and continue to conflict with Victorian cultural conventions of female identity and behaviour. The **Bildungsroman** plot is concerned with educating the protagonist into his/her appropriate gender role, but Maggie hungers for 'masculine' education and in this way resists her education into femininity. George Eliot's disruption of the Bildungsroman narrative structure seems to mirror Maggie's resistance. The ending of the novel marks a final generic shift from the Bildungsroman structure which should deal with Maggie and Tom's increasing maturity. Instead, the narrative is cyclical and apparently fulfils Maggie's desire of a return to an Edenic unity with Tom.

THEMES

The themes in this novel are characterised by a tension between the real and ideal, the public and private, the individual and society.

ORIGINS AND EVOLUTION

George Eliot was greatly influenced by the theories of evolution which were emerging in the mid nineteenth century (see Historical Background – Thought and Belief). They brought about an upheaval in beliefs and religious certainties, central to which was the questioning of human origins and of the Genesis myth of Christian belief. *The Mill on the Floss* explores this concern with origins, and George Eliot develops this theme through a motif common in Victorian literature – a return to childhood. The early childhood of Tom and Maggie, which exists prior to the beginning of this novel, is remembered as Edenic. The obvious biblical overtones of this memory are also combined, however, with the more pagan depictions of the power of the River Floss, which is the site of Maggie's memory of union with Tom. The river is a kind of maternal symbol (its watery, life-giving function allying it with the womb), and, with its connection to the sea, is also the location for the first life forms, a kind of womb of all life.

Kinship and heredity are also constant themes in this novel. The Dodson sisters consistently assert the superiority of their genes and familial traditions. Much is made of Maggie and Tom's different heredity, with repeated assumptions made about what this means for the continuation of the familial line and for each as an individual. Throughout the novel the theme of evolution (in the sense of species evolution and social evolution) is debated and George Eliot seeks to reconcile her readers to the new theories. Bonds, especially between humans and dogs (Maggie and Yap, Bob and Mumps, Lucy and Minny), are important relationships, and animal imagery is used to convey aspects of character: Tom is likened to a 'gosling' (p. 84), Lucy to a 'pretty spaniel' (p. 495), and Maggie to a 'small Shetland pony' (p. 61) and a 'Skye terrier' (p. 64). More than this, though, animal imagery signals human membership of the animal kingdom and the more instinctive, uninhibited human responses which children exhibit (for example, Tom and Maggie, p. 91), but which are repressed in adulthood. Animal imagery also signals the dangerous animal aspects of human nature, as the predatory imagery used to explore Wakem's motivations demonstrates (p. 338).

However, George Eliot clearly does not endorse a totally free expression of all animal instincts and she creates Maggie's dilemma as a focus for the debate about what it is to be human. Maggie is torn between following her instinctive, sensual and animal instincts and adhering to a sense of duty and responsibility. Maggie's 'animal' behaviour, as she dances with Yap the dog, is acceptable while she is a child, but Luke's admonition becomes a prophetic warning about following her animal instincts as an adult: 'you'll make yourself giddy an' tumble down i' the dirt' (pp. 79-80). This is metaphorically what does happen when she follows her sexual instincts with Stephen and falls into the 'dirt' of a ruined reputation. Maggie and Stephen also debate this issue at the crucial point when Maggie refuses to marry him. He tries to persuade her that 'natural law surmounts every other' and that their sexual attraction should not be denied (p. 601). However, Maggie responds with a question central to the moral evolution of society: 'If the past is not to bind us, where can duty lie? We should have no law but the inclination of the moment' (pp. 601–2).

The theme of social evolution and the emergence of a **humanistic** moral system is developed by George Eliot's reference to the interconnection of characters' lives: web imagery suggests this

interconnection, as do direct comments. For Tom this connection is
frustrating and after his father has attacked Mr Wakem, he broods on the
fact that his life is entangled with the lives of others:

> Apparently the mingled thread in the web of their life was so curiously twisted
> together that there could be no joy without a sorrow coming close upon it. Tom
> was dejected by the thought that his exemplary effort must always be baffled by the
> wrong-doing of others (p. 462)

George Eliot also explores society's slow organic change, described in
social evolutionary theories, with her acknowledgement of the crucial
continuum of past, present and future. St Ogg's develops slowly through
historical and mythical time; in fact, there is some criticism of this town
because it relies too heavily on the past and on tradition and is not
developing at all (as the parallels with the ruined village on the banks of
the Rhône suggest, p. 362). Maggie and Tom's extinction can be seen as
a result of being too closely bound to this static society. The catastrophic
flood does bring about a change in keeping with gradualist theories. The
change is only slight in terms of the landscape, the flood 'had left little
visible trace on the earth, five years after', but the deaths of Maggie and
Tom have affected the social evolution of this community (p. 656).

CONSTRAINT AND ESCAPE

The narrow society in which she lives (epitomised by the Dodson sisters
with their miserly materialism and strict and inhuman moral code)
constrains Maggie psychologically, physically and spiritually. Like many
other heroines trapped in a limiting social context, Maggie finds ways to
escape. She forgets her reality by escaping into her imagination, which is
stimulated by literature, and into a daydream state which is induced by
the sound of the Mill, the river and music (see Patterns of Imagery,
Metaphors, Symbols). Maggie also considers the conventional escape
from mundane and limited home life for women through marriage to
Philip or Stephen. However, George Eliot will not permit this escape for
her heroine, and we realise that it would be a mistake for Maggie to marry
either of these men, since neither is fully compatible with her.

Eventually, this longing and need for escape become a destructive
desire for oblivion, as increasingly the social pressures and Maggie's own

sense of what is morally right prevent the fulfilment of her desires and ambitions. Finally, the conflict is too great and Maggie's wish for extinction is met by the powerful flood which breaks the banks of the river and metaphorically obliterates the social, personal and moral barriers between Tom and Maggie.

EDUCATION

There were several educational reforms made during George Eliot's life, which were intended to broaden and make more uniform the educational provision for boys and girls of all classes. Increasingly, women were being included at the higher levels of education and George Eliot donated £50 to the fund used to establish Girton College for women at Cambridge University. However, her attitude to women's education was equivocal: on one hand she agreed that there ought to be educational and social equality for women, on the other, she argued that women's feminine character (women's particular capacity for moral influence, gentleness and tenderness) might be lost, and women become unsexed, through formal education.

Education in *The Mill on the Floss* is both formal and cultural, and the different education that Maggie and Tom receive is supposed to be that best suited to their sex and gender identity, and to their social role. For neither is this the case. Tom's formal education leads to his humiliation and he leaves with only a veneer of classical learning; it is completely at odds with the career that he wants to follow and for which he is suited. It is only when he is in the public world of employment, having received appropriate instruction for this work, that he can excel, utilising his skills to full effect. His social education does suit his character, but in fact encourages the development of what are seen to be the more negative facets of his personality – his self-righteousness, his single-mindedness, his limited moral sense, his arrogance and cruelty. Mrs Tulliver encourages his domineering behaviour, and Mr Deane promotes him, expressing admiration of his progress, although voicing concern about his single-minded preoccupation with work.

Maggie, on the other hand, would have gained considerably from the kind of education at which Tom fails. For her to desire such an education is seen as an aberration and a defiance of her femininity.

Victorian medical science considered women to be unsuited to extensive intellectual activity since their loss of menstrual blood meant the vital loss of mental energy too. Maggie's desire for 'masculine' knowledge is related using images drawn from the biblical story of Eve's sinful acquisition of the forbidden fruit. Eve-like, Maggie 'began to nibble at this thick-rinded fruit of the tree of knowledge' (p. 380). This imagery conveys the extent of Maggie's affront to social convention and the rebellious and sinful implications such a desire carries. In doing this 'She rebelled against her lot' and feared 'it was not difficult for her to become a demon' (p. 380). Later, her hunger for pleasure, and for intellectual and sensual stimulation is channelled through her equally sinful sexual desire for Stephen.

The formal education Maggie does receive is glossed over, possibly suggesting the triviality of the education considered appropriate to young ladies. Maggie's social education is seen in all its painful detail. The warring with her mother over her hair and her dress, being hurt by Mr Stelling's sexist views of clever women, and her father's collusion with dominant social conventions all educate Maggie into accepting her inferior status as a woman in **patriarchal** society. This 'training' inhibits her development as an individual and leads to self-destructive internal conflict.

PATTERNS OF IMAGERY, METAPHORS, SYMBOLS

Much of the imagery that George Eliot employs in this novel is closely related to the themes. Animal imagery and biblical imagery have already been mentioned. In *Darwin's Plots: Evolutionary Narrative in Darwin, George Eliot and Nineteenth-Century Fiction* (Ark Paperbacks, 1983), Gillian Beer argues that figurative language was used by Victorian writers to express a fascination with experience beyond the domain of the rational. She further argues that '[s]ymbol and metaphor, as opposed to analysis, can allow insight without consequences because perceptions are not stabilised and categorised. They allow us fleetingly to inhabit contradictory experience without moralising it' (p. 14). In being free from the implications of Freudian theory, whereby imagery is now subject to rapid interpretation and instantly reveals unconscious desires, Victorian novelists used metaphor as a means of indirectly expressing ideas which may have been the cause for censure, such as ideas about sexuality.

Two of the most prominent patterns of imagery in *The Mill on the Floss* are those concerned with water and music.

WATER

The water imagery, especially that related to the river, is used throughout the novel to metaphorically represent a more organic and spiritual dimension of life, a more natural and free-flowing expression of feeling. Further, water imagery provides George Eliot with a means of indirectly articulating emotions and desires that contemporary mores would not allow; water imagery expresses unconscious or culturally repressed desires.

Although George Eliot undertook a large amount of research and travelling in order to find a river and setting suitable to use as a real basis for her fictional River Floss (and found it in Lincolnshire), the Floss also takes on a mythical and metaphorical meaning. Comment on it recalls not only Noah's flood, but also the superstition about the river's vengeance when Dorlcote Mill changes hands. It takes on great symbolic meaning as the river of life and of destruction. It is central to the relationship between Maggie and Tom: it is the location of Maggie's first and lasting memory of unity with Tom; and water imagery expresses their different characters and the relationship between them (compare the first sentence of the novel and their different responses to their impoverished state, p. 380). Finally it is the reason for Maggie's attempted heroic rescue of Tom, the site of his recognition of her worth, and ultimately the place of their deaths.

Water imagery is especially connected with Maggie: from destroying her curls with water as a child to following her adult desires as she drifts downstream with Stephen, water signals Maggie's rebellion. A river analogy is used to discuss Maggie's destiny and, in its central role in the myth of the naming of St Ogg's, the river is also closely associated with the fulfilment of a woman's desire (p. 514–5). The Virgin, disguised in rags, longs to cross the river, but it is only Ogg who has respect enough for her 'heart's need' to ferry her across (p. 182). This association of the river and a woman's desire becomes heightened in the developing relationship between Maggie and Stephen. The river represents the current of sexual desire and passion, the force of Maggie's temptation, the suspension of her awareness and moral conscience and, simultaneously, the danger of all of this. It seems significant that Stephen arrives for the first illicit meeting with Maggie via the river (stressed by the repetition of this fact, p. 518). Rowing down the river with Stephen, Maggie feels that they are in an 'enchanted haze' which is timeless and the flow of the river seems to act as the agent of her 'fall' as it causes her to drift downstream with him (p. 589). On the steamer, water imagery conveys her feelings of freedom from her ties and responsibilities, and from the struggle between her desire and conscience:

> But now nothing was distinct to her: she was being lulled to sleep with that soft stream still flowing over her, with those delicious visions melting and fading like the wondrous aërial land of the west (p. 595)

MUSIC

Music too has the effect of transporting Maggie out of her reality and into a state of rapture and enchantment. Both literally and metaphorically it expresses her longings and desires, as well as her need to escape the mundane and limited scope of her life. Music stimulates Maggie's imagination when she is a child and she responds in an ecstatic way. The carols sung on Christmas Eve fill her with wonder, despite Tom's efforts to deflate her enthralment with the prosaic reality that the singers are ordinary people that they know. To Maggie they are 'the vision of angels resting on the parted cloud' who give rise to 'supernatural singing' (p. 224). Music is one of the things she feels most deprived of after her father's bankruptcy, and musical imagery is used to express the awe she feels in reading another reader's response to the book by Thomas à Kempis. Her adoption of the doctrine of self-renunciation is her response to her changed circumstances; this is paralleled with music in that it too is a means of escaping her mundane reality.

Discussion of their similar appreciation of music is what draws Maggie to Philip. His voice as he persuades her to meet him again in the Red Deeps is 'sweet music', and despite the warning voice of her conscience, she cannot resist his entreaty: 'Yet the music would swell out again, like chimes borne onward by a recurrent breeze, persuading her that the wrong lay all in the faults and weaknesses of others' (p. 399). In Maggie's relationship with Stephen, the musical imagery expresses the sexual temptation and desire between the two lovers. We are told that after years of deprivation, music for Maggie is 'a more pregnant, passionate language', and an aspect of her 'passionate sensibility' (p. 514). She also tells Lucy that it 'seems to infuse strength' into her body and 'ideas' into her brain, releasing her from the 'weight' of responsibility and her mundane life (p. 496). Later, Stephen also uses music as a language with which to communicate his desire to Maggie (p. 583).

However, Maggie's response to music is also dangerous, and even early in her life her relationship with music signals her divergence from feminine norms. Her mother, the voice of convention, complains about her behaviour and associates it with madness: 'I'm sure the child's half a idiot i' some things [...] she [...] 'ull sit down on the floor i' the sunshine an' plait her hair an' sing to herself like a Bedlam creatur" (p. 60). The sensual effect of Stephen's singing on Maggie is conveyed by the sexual suggestion of the words used to describe her response: as he begins to sing Maggie has a 'sudden thrill', she is described as 'quivering' and 'clasping', as 'her eyes dilated and brightened' (p. 532). George Eliot uses Maggie's differing response to the singing of Philip and Stephen to clearly show where Maggie's true passion lies. She is 'touched not thrilled' by Philip's song (p. 533), but Stephen's 'saucy energy', by contrast, has a tremendous impact on her: 'in spite of her resistance to the spirit of the song and to the singer, [Maggie] was taken hold of and shaken by the invisible influence – was borne along by a wave too strong for her' (p. 534). This combination of literal music and water imagery signals both Maggie's ecstasy and desire, and the danger of this. It anticipates the fate of Maggie and Stephen as both are carried away by desires and the by flow of the river.

TIME

The fact that George Eliot set the majority of her fiction in the past has been seen by some critics as simply nostalgia for a lost and better time. However, this setting does have a thematic purpose in that contemporary readers, well aware of the changes in society, are required to bring a historical perspective to their interpretation, and to draw contrasts between the past and the present. In periods of rapid change, George Eliot suggests, it is crucial to remember where we have come from in order to understand where we are. Like other writers of this period, George Eliot addresses the concerns of her time, though she does so through a gaze into the past.

The action of *The Mill on the Floss* takes place between 1829 and 1839, with the conclusion set five years later. Time moves unevenly in the novel: George Eliot may dwell for several chapters on a single day (Book 1, Chapter 8–11) or gloss over the passing of years with only a brief comment (Maggie's two years at school with Lucy, for instance, Book 2, Chapter 7), or even leave a gap in her narrative (between Books 5 and 6 there is a gap of two years). In places, time also seems to be subjective, for example, minutes seem like hours to Maggie crying in the attic and this reflects Maggie's childlike experience of rejection (p. 89). Similarly, Mr Tulliver in his illness does not realise that time is passing and is shocked to find the family's circumstances radically altered when he recovers. The watchers at his sickbed experience a sense of double time: if time were measured only by Mr Tulliver's painfully slow recovery it would barely seem to move, but it passes frighteningly fast as the day approaches for the settlement of their debts (p. 329).

Time also moves between the past and the present as characters recall and dwell on their memories at key times in the narrative. Gillian Beer has commented that 'the narrative is arranged like a memory with crystal-clear episodes of recall' which give insights into the feelings, motivations and psychological development of the characters ('Beyond Determinism: George Eliot and Virginia Woolf', in *Women and Writing About Women*, M. Jacobus, ed., Croom Helm Ltd., 1979, p. 87). These 'crystal-clear episodes' include Maggie's memory of holding hands with Tom by the side of the Floss, Mr Tulliver's memory of the day the malthouse was completed and his thoughts on the generations of Tullivers who have lived there, and Philip's memory of meeting Maggie at school. George Eliot's narrative also moves back into historical and mythic time in order to contextualise the story of Maggie and Tom and to develop her theme of the gradual development of human society.

PART FOUR

TEXTUAL ANALYSIS

TEXT 1 (PAGES 79–80)

'Hegh, hegh, Miss, you'll make yourself giddy an' tumble down i' the dirt,' said Luke, the head miller, a tall broad-shouldered man of forty, black-eyed and black-haired, subdued by a general mealiness, like an auricula.

Maggie paused in her whirling and said, staggering a little, 'O no, it doesn't make me giddy. Luke, may I go into the mill with you?'

Maggie loved to linger in the great spaces of the mill, and often came out with her black hair powdered to a soft whiteness that made her dark eyes flash out with new fire. The resolute din, the unresting motion of the great stones giving her a dim delicious awe as at the presence of an uncontrollable force, the meal for ever pouring, pouring, the fine white powder softening all surfaces and making the very spider-nets look like faery lace-work, the sweet pure scent of the meal – all helped to make Maggie feel that the mill was a little world apart from her outside everyday life. The spiders were especially a subject of speculation with her: she wondered if they had any relations outside the mill, for in that case there must be a painful difficulty in their family intercourse: a fat and floury spider, accustomed to take his fly well dusted with meal, must suffer a little at a cousin's table where the fly was *au naturel*, and the lady spiders must be mutually shocked at each other's appearance. But the part of the mill she liked best was the topmost story – the corn-hutch where there were the great heaps of grain which she could sit on and slide down continually. She was in the habit of taking this recreation as she conversed with Luke, to whom she was very communicative, wishing him to think well of her understanding, as her father did.

Maggie has just come down from the attic where she has been violently wreaking vengeance on her Fetish (a wooden doll) for what she sees as the injustices that she suffers because she is a girl and, therefore, obliged to be feminine. A chain of events had led her to this state: she was not allowed to go with her father to collect Tom because her best bonnet would get wet, then she wet her hair in a basin of water in rebellion against having it femininely curled, she was then chastised for her naughtiness and her mother threatened to tell her aunts about Maggie's behaviour. However, as 'a sudden beam of sunshine' comes into the attic, Maggie's mood changes and she goes to dance with Yap in the yard, ecstatic that Tom is coming home.

In this passage from Book 1, Chapter 4, we are given an insight into Maggie's character as a child and this provides us with a key to aspects of her adult character. As we have seen before, she is keen to be recognised as intelligent and here, with typical childlike pride in her accomplishments, she wants Luke to 'think well of her understanding, as her father did'. George Eliot was praised for her authentic representation of childhood and Maggie's immense pleasure in sliding down the 'great heaps of grain' is evocative of childhood joy that many of her readers would be able to recall. Maggie's denial that whirling around with Yap will make her 'giddy', spoken even as she is 'staggering a little', is also typical of a child. Her enjoyment of sliding on the grain is a mark of her tomboyish nature, and there are many other instances where we see that she would indeed like to be a boy like Tom is.

Similarly childlike, and characteristic of Maggie, is the way that she creates another imaginary world into which she can momentarily escape from the real world. Lucy admires this imaginative quality, although Tom resents it. George Eliot's use of **alliteration** in 'dim, delicious' emphasises the power that the motion of the millstones has for Maggie: it is 'an uncontrollable force' which mesmerises her. We see her similarly mesmerised at the beginning of the novel as she watches the motion of the mill wheel. The repetition of 'pouring' gives us a sense of the constant movement of the grain and allows us to identify with Maggie as she is lulled into this fantasy world. Later her continual sliding emphasises the association of Maggie's whole being, body and mind, with the unresting millstones and with this place.

Here she whimsically speculates on the familial relations of the spiders who live in the mill. Her anthropomorphic depiction of their activities is humorously childlike, but also reveals her discomfort with family tensions and her difficulty in fitting into her own family. In particular Maggie considers the mealtime experiences of the different branches of the arachnid family and the 'painful difficulty in their family intercourse'. Food is very central to a child's world and it is to Maggie and Tom; one of the major arguments they have is over a jam puff, and it is the custards that tempt Maggie into the dining room after she has cut her hair. However, food becomes a focus for animosity and division between the siblings and between the Dodson and Tulliver branches of the family, as is evident in Mrs Glegg's scathing comments about the excessive food at the Tulliver's party, for example.

In this brief fantasy speculation, Maggie also seems to play out her resistance to the feminine norms imposed on her. Her resentment at the repeated comparisons made between her and her angelic, 'naturally' feminine cousin Lucy could be inferred from this fantasy. She remarks on the shocking differences between the appearance of the floury lady spiders from the mill and their cousins, 'the lady spiders must be mutually shocked at each other's appearance.' The fact that Maggie emerges from the mill 'with her black hair powdered to a soft whiteness' clearly identifies her with one branch of this spider family, and the fact that the shock is mutual demonstrates the way that Maggie sees femininity and conformity as being as shocking as others consider her unfemininity and rebelliousness to be. The tension between expressing her individuality and conforming to social conventions will be the central dilemma of Maggie's adult life.

In this novel, George Eliot creates a sense of continuity between childhood experience and character and adult identity and destiny. Many aspects of her character revealed here are developed and transformed as Maggie grows into adulthood. We see that as a child, the stimulation of her senses and her imagination is exhilarating; when she emerges from the mill covered in flour 'her dark eyes flash out with new fire.' Later it is the river, the driving force of the mill wheel, and music (linked in theme and image to the river) which have a similar, though more dangerous, effect on her. Literally they arouse her senses and desires and give rise to a sensation of detachment from the duties and responsibilities of the real world, a development of the imaginary worlds that she creates in her childhood. The river and music are also used metaphorically by the author to articulate the uncontrollable nature and the powerful force of Maggie's desires.

Luke's warning here that she will make herself 'giddy an' tumble down i' the dirt' if she continues to whirl around in her dance with Yap is prophetic. George Eliot's conception of **realism**, like William Wordsworth's, involved using the 'language of men', and giving voice to those not usually heard in literature. Here she not only uses the words of a working-class man spoken in a regional dialect, but also gives his words an important function. His comment later in this chapter that 'Things out o' natur niver thrive' is similarly profound (p. 82). Later when Maggie follows her (sexual) animal instincts, she does metaphorically fall into the 'dirt' of a ruined reputation and scandal. Further, the assessment she makes of the effect of her whirling dance is inaccurate, and we are alerted to the fact that later she will not be able to completely assess the effect of her whirlwind romance with Stephen, or fully acknowledge her feelings and motivation (the way she feels about Philip, for example).

TEXT 2   (PAGES 339–40)

Prosperous men take a little vengeance now and then, as they take a diversion, when it comes easily in their way and is no hindrance to business; and such small unimpassioned revenges have an enormous effect in life, running through all degrees of pleasant infliction, blocking the fit men out of places, and blackening characters in unpremeditated talk. Still more, to see people who have been only insignificantly offensive to us, reduced in life and humiliated without any special efforts of ours is apt to have a soothing, flattering influence: Providence, or some other prince of this world, it appears, has undertaken the task of retribution for us; and really, by an agreeable constitution of things, our enemies, somehow, *don't* prosper.

Wakem was not without this parenthetic vindictiveness towards the uncomplimentary miller, and now Mrs Tulliver had put the notion into his head it presented itself to him as a pleasure to do the very thing that would cause Mr Tulliver the most deadly mortification, and a pleasure of a complex kind, not made up of crude malice but mingling with it the relish of self-approbation. To see an enemy humiliated gives a certain contentment, but this is jejune compared with the highly blent satisfaction of seeing him humiliated by your benevolent action of concession on his behalf. That is a sort of revenge which falls into the scale of virtue, and Wakem was not without an intention of keeping that scale respectably filled. He had once had the pleasure of putting an old enemy of his into one of the St Ogg's almshouses, to the rebuilding of which he had given a large subscription; and here was an opportunity of providing for another by making him his own servant. Such things give a completeness to prosperity, and contribute elements of agreeable consciousness that are not dreamed of by that short-sighted over-heated vindictiveness, which goes out of its way to wreak itself in direct injury. And Tulliver with his rough tongue filed by a sense of obligation, would make a better servant than any chance fellow who was cap-in-hand for a situation. Tulliver was known to be a man of proud honesty, and Wakem was too acute not to believe in the existence of honesty.

This passage, from the middle of the extended discussion of Mr Wakem's decision to buy Dorlcote Mill (Book 2, Chapter 7), is a good illustration of the analytical style George Eliot uses frequently in *The Mill on the Floss* to lay bare a character's motivation. Discussion of the relationship between Mr Tulliver and Mr Wakem prior to this passage has drawn on two analogies: one concerning the food chain, whereby the larger fish (Wakem) devours the smaller fish (Tulliver) as a matter of course, and another concerning political rivalry. Both help to build up a sense of Wakem's cool detachment and a sense of his revenge being somehow 'natural', or at least part of human nature. In this section George Eliot exposes Wakem as a cold-hearted opportunist and as a hypocrite.

The passage begins with a generalised observation of the way that revenge is merely an entertainment, 'a diversion', for prosperous men. However, the effect of such diversions is 'enormous' on those suffering as a result. The paradoxical phrase 'pleasant infliction' sums up the difference in the experience of the person enacting the revenge and the person who suffers the consequences. This distinction is elaborated with the contrasts established immediately after it. The result for those having revenge taken upon them is the 'blocking' of careers, and the 'blackening' of reputations. The **alliteration** of the harsh 'bl' consonant sounds at the beginning of these verbs emphasises the impact of such consequences. This differs starkly from the 'soothing, flattering' effect for those enacting the revenge. These contrasts continue and become more emphatic in the following paragraph as the true malicious vindictiveness of Mr Wakem is fully exposed.

However, before the reader is allowed to rush into any quick and easy judgements of Wakem's actions, the narrative technique George Eliot employs forces us to stop and consider our own involvement in similar acts of revenge. By the slippage from the objective third-person narration of 'Prosperous men' and 'they', to the subjective first-person narration of 'us' and 'our', George Eliot involves us by requiring that we consider our own behaviour (see **omniscient narrator**). By insisting on the reader's collusion in the generalisations being made, she forces us to recognise the temptation of being able to punish an enemy without effort, and with responsibility apparently taken out of our hands by the workings of fate or Providence. George Eliot frequently subtly slips between these two narrative modes in this novel, thus complicating our moral response by alerting us to our own fallibility.

When the analysis moves on to the specific motivation of Wakem and we recoil from his malicious hypocrisy, we are at least judging him in a more self-aware and honest way. This further highlights the fact that it is Wakem's dishonesty and deception that really end any possibility of our sympathy for his actions. His plan to increase his reputation as a respectable, benevolent and magnanimous man (as he has done before), whilst simultaneously enacting his almost sadistic revenge is too much to tolerate. The descriptions of the benefits and pleasures he will gain are repulsive, as in his 'crude malice ... mingling with it the relish of self-approbation'.

The contrasts in the experiences of being the revenger and being the recipient of an act of revenge become more vividly differentiated in this paragraph. The recipient suffers 'deadly mortification', and is 'humiliated' and made a 'servant'; the revenger experiences 'pleasure' and 'highly blent satisfaction'. Our hostility towards Wakem mounts as the paragraph develops until, finally, his malicious wielding of power is expressed in a painful metaphor, evoking the agony that the proud and honest miller will suffer: 'Tulliver with his rough tongue filed by a sense of obligation'. Our sympathy at this point is wholly with Mr Tulliver.

However, sympathy has been building for Mr Tulliver throughout this paragraph. Although we may dislike Mr Tulliver's outspoken anger and vindictiveness, here it provides a clear contrast to Wakem's cunning and malice. The fact that he is mildly described as being merely 'uncomplimentary', contributes to our sense that Mr Tulliver does not deserve such a harsh revenge as Wakem is taking. Further, our knowledge of his life-threatening illness makes George Eliot's choice of the phrase 'deadly mortification' all the more menacing. Finally, as much as we may see the futility of Mr Tulliver's 'short-sighted, over-heated vindictiveness' which only injures himself, we know also of his generosity of spirit and admire his unshakeable honesty, a quality which is underlined by the fact that Wakem recognises it too and intends to use it to his own advantage.

TEXT 3 (PAGES 469–70)

The well-furnished drawing-room, with the open grand piano and the pleasant outlook down a sloping garden to a boat-house by the side of the Floss, is Mr Deane's. The neat little lady in mourning, whose light brown ringlets are falling over the coloured embroidery with which her fingers are busy, is of course Lucy Deane; and the fine young man who is leaning down from his chair to snap the scissors in the extremely abbreviated face of the 'King Charles' lying on the young lady's feet, is no other than Mr Stephen Guest, whose diamond ring, attar of roses, and air of nonchalant leisure at twelve o' clock in the day are the graceful and odoriferous result of the largest oil-mill and the most extensive wharf in St Ogg's. There is an apparent triviality in the action with the scissors, but your discernment perceives at once that there is a design in it which makes it eminently worthy of a large-headed, long-limbed young man; for you see that Lucy wants the scissors and is compelled, reluctant as she may be, to shake her ringlets back, raise her soft hazel eyes, smile playfully down on the face that is so very nearly on a level with her knee, and holding out her little shell-pink palm, to say

'My scissors, please, if you can renounce the great pleasure of persecuting my poor Minny.'

The foolish scissors have slipped too far over the knuckles, it seems, and Hercules holds out his entrapped fingers hopelessly.

'Confound the scissors! The oval lies the wrong way. Please, draw them off for me.'

'Draw them off with your other hand,' says Miss Lucy, roguishly.

'O but that's my left hand: I'm not left-handed.' Lucy laughs and the scissors are drawn off with gentle touches from tiny tips, which naturally dispose Mr Stephen for a repetition *da capo*. Accordingly, he watches for the release of the scissors that he may get them into his possession again.

This scene opens the third book of the novel. Two years have passed since Mr Tulliver's death and George Eliot makes us aware that although the majority of the protagonists are the same, time has moved on. The setting is quite different, signalling also a change in focus in terms of the subject matter. The emphasis on family ties will now shift to an exploration of the complexities of romantic relationships, although family bonds as well as the forces of social convention, which in part dictate relationships between men and women, will remain important.

Several early critics and reviewers complained that this final book was not in keeping with the previous two. David Carroll sums this up: 'reviewers felt both shocked and betrayed. After being taken at leisurely pace through two volumes of apparently commonplace life at Dorlcote Mill they were suddenly plunged into the terrible conflicts of passion and conscience in volume three' (David Carroll, ed., *George Eliot: The Critical Heritage*, Routledge and Kegan Paul, 1971, p. 13). Swinburne was perhaps the most vehement in his assessment of this final book as 'the patent flaw ... the flagrant blemish ... a cancer in the very bosom, a gangrene in the very flesh ... corrosive and incurable' (Swinburne, in Carroll, p. 165). Although the opening of this book is on the surface quite calm, relaxed and harmless, even here the reader is alerted to more dangerous undercurrents of character, action and theme which are soon to become more apparent.

The opening of this chapter is a good example of George Eliot's pictorial style, which she employed also at the beginning of the novel. There she paints a landscape, with Dorlcote Mill and Maggie foregrounded, and here she paints an interior scene of upper-middle-class leisure and ease. It is as if we are looking at the set of a play of which this is the final act. Not only are we introduced to two of the key actors, but the first sentence points out the important 'prop', the piano, and the symbolic locations of the garden with its boathouse, and the Floss, which are visible in the background. Music will be important in the complex relationships that develop, and the river and boating fulfil important functions, providing opportunities for romantic moments and metaphorically expressing the intensity and the danger of Maggie and Stephen's desire. This scene, then, assembles most of the elements for the final complication and denouement of this drama.

The opening paragraph describes the young lovers, Lucy and Stephen, as if they are posed for our almost voyeuristic gaze on them. Once 'animated' their interaction provides us with an insight into their relationship. Lucy Deane continues to be the angelic ideal of femininity: the 'neat little lady' is 'of course' Lucy Deane. She is, as ever, associated with light, 'light brown ringlets', with gentleness, 'soft hazel eyes', and with delicacy 'her little shell-pink palm'. She is embroidering, a traditionally feminine occupation, whilst her would-be fiancé sits romantically at her feet. As well as the development of this relationship with Stephen, there has been another significant change in her life too, as her mourning clothes suggest. We discover later that her mother has died.

Stephen Guest was unfavourably received by early reviewers and critics, and it is not hard to see why from this brief but sharply focused introduction of him. He is depicted as a provincial dandy, bejewelled and perfumed, and his idle detachment from the source of his wealth is implicitly criticised here, as it was in the only earlier mention of him by Mr Deane. **Irony** is used to highlight the incongruity of this manly man and his actions. Compound adjectives are used to create a sense of his solidity and size, 'large-headed, long-limbed', and this seems incompatible with his 'apparent triviality' with the scissors. George Eliot's reference to him as 'Hercules' also ironically reinforces the picture of a man whose physique is at odds with the fact that his fingers are trapped in the scissors. The **alliteration** of 'Hercules, holds' and 'hopelessly' emphasises this incongruity by drawing attention to the contradiction of our expectations – we do not expect a manly hero to need rescuing from his entrapment in a pair of scissors! Although the adjective 'foolish' is applied here to the scissors, we can see that it is really an apt description for his frivolous actions.

Clearly we are not meant to consider Stephen to be simply an ineffectual dandy, however, and his cruelty as he snips the scissors in Minny's face suggests a disturbing undercurrent to his actions and character. His behaviour towards the dog is especially striking since human relationships with dogs have been important literally and thematically so far in this novel. As with the majority of George Eliot's characters, Stephen is far more complex than he would at first appear, and the narrative intervention is one way that we realise this. As readers we are invited to collude, 'your discernment perceives', with the fact that Stephen's actions with the scissors are only apparently trivial because he is really engaged in the serious activity of flirting with Lucy. However, this triviality is only 'apparent' in another sense too: his teasing flirtation is also designed to gain power and attract attention to himself. In this respect his action *is* 'worthy' and appropriate to this physically and financially powerful young man. Thus the reader is at once flatteringly invited to collude in the **ironic** treatment of him, and made to realise the more dangerous aspect of his character.

As a result of Stephen's flirtatious behaviour, Lucy is 'compelled' although 'reluctant' to ask for her scissors; here this is obviously playful and Lucy's initial transgression of her usually compliant behaviour, in refusing 'roguishly' to remove the scissors, is not serious. However, when Stephen later flirts with Maggie the intensity of their emotions as well as their transgression of social convention is far more dangerous. Comically here he gets his fingers trapped, but later, his flirtation leads to him being 'entrapped ... hopelessly' with far more dramatic consequences. Here Lucy does remove the scissors and the description of her 'gentle touches from tiny tips' emphasises that this action is an expression of her femininity; it also encourages Stephen to repeat his actions. The musical term, '*da capo*', is significant since it is through music that Stephen and Lucy's bond has been sealed and, as we see later in this chapter with Stephen's choice of Haydn's *The Creation*, music gives us an insight into the dynamics of their relationship. Music is also central to the attraction and increasingly intense desire between Maggie and Stephen, articulating their passion and weakening their resistance to temptation.

It is into this setting of luxury, romance, music and pleasure that Maggie is soon to enter. It offers a marked contrast to the impoverished Tulliver household and an even greater one to Maggie's school life. It is not difficult, therefore, to see why she is so overwhelmed. The presence of this charming, flirtatious masculine man represents an obvious temptation for the inexperienced Maggie, a danger predicted by Philip's imaginary scene (closely resembling this one) in which Maggie would steal her fair cousin's lover (p. 433).

PART FIVE

BACKGROUND

GEORGE ELIOT

Born in 1819 (in the same year as Queen Victoria) in Nuneaton, Warwickshire, Mary Anne Evans (later Mary Ann, Marian, Mrs Lewes and George Eliot) was the youngest daughter of her father's second marriage to Christiana Pearson. Her family was lower middle-class, though her father was a very successful man who, by the time George Eliot was born, had risen socially from the position of carpenter to a powerful position as land agent for the Newdigate family on the Arbury Estate in Warwickshire. George Eliot's relationship with her mother was not an affectionate one, and her mother's strict and efficient attitude to her children's welfare left little scope for a close relationship to develop. The relationship between Maggie and Mrs Tulliver in *The Mill on the Floss* may well be an expression of the distance George Eliot felt from her own mother. Christiana also had three sisters who may well have been the models for the Dodson sisters. On the other hand, George Eliot worshipped her father and her older brother, Isaac. Her sonnet sequence called 'Brother and Sister' (1869) testifies to the intense bond she felt with her brother, who at the point at which she wrote the sonnets had not communicated with her for about fourteen years. The sonnets are set in the period of 1824 to 1825 when George Eliot would have been four or five, a period which for her character Maggie is also one of blissful union with her brother Tom.

In many ways George Eliot's early life was a privileged one. Griff House on the edge of the Arbury estate, where she lived until she was twenty-one, came to represent an idyllic locus for happiness. The rural settings of the past in many of her novels draw on this place and time. The education she received was not typical for a girl and young woman of her social class, and at the two boarding schools (which she attended from 1824 onwards) and at Miss Franklin's School in Coventry (where she went in 1832) George Eliot excelled intellectually and linguistically. She studied French and German, Music, English Literature and Composition and later, when she lived at home after her mother's death in 1836, her father provided for her tuition in Italian and German.

It was in 1828 at Wallington Boarding School that George Eliot met Maria Lewis, her teacher and later close friend. An Evangelical Christian, Maria Lewis had a profound effect on George Eliot's intellectual, emotional and spiritual development and George Eliot adopted an Evangelical belief until her early twenties. For a while she renounced all pleasures, including music and literature, though towards the end of the 1830s she did begin to read things that challenged her Calvinist beliefs (for example, the poetry of Lord Byron and William Wordsworth, and geological explanations of origins). Isaac married, replaced his father as land agent for the Arbury Estate and came to live at Griff House, and George Eliot and her father moved to Coventry in 1841. Here her system of belief was completely transformed by her close friendship with Charles and Caroline Bray. She now began to see Christianity as a cultural construction and was influenced by Charles Hennell (Caroline's brother)'s ground-breaking study *An Inquiry into the Origins of Christianity* (1838). As a consequence she refused to attend church with her conventionally devout father, causing a long-term breach only resolved at the time of his death (1849). After being sent to live for a short time with her brother at Griff House, George Eliot reached a compromise with her father: she would attend church if he did not question her about her beliefs.

In 1844 George Eliot began her translation of David Friedrich Strauss's *The Life of Jesus* (1835). Several qualified writers had already found this task too daunting and difficult, but with determination and daily hard work George Eliot finished the translation in two years. This work, as well as her translation in 1854 of Ludwig Feuerbach's *The Essence of Christianity* (1841), published in 1854, brought George Eliot increasingly into contact with many leading intellectuals. These contacts increased when, after her father's death and a year spent in Switzerland, she worked as assistant editor for the radical and intellectual journal the *Westminster Review* (between 1852 and 1854). In January 1851 she began to lodge with John Chapman, the editor of the *Westminster Review*, his wife, his children and his mistress, who was acting as governess to the children. It is not clear what the relationship was between Chapman and Marian (as she called herself after 1850, though also Polly and Pollian), however, there was great sexual tension in the house and Marian was eventually forced to leave in March 1851, only to return later that year. She eventually left in September 1853. Her hard work made the *Westminster Review* one of the leading intellectual journals of the day.

In 1851 George Eliot met George Henry Lewes. He was married but could not obtain a divorce because he had accepted his wife and her lover's child as his own. In 1854 George Eliot and Lewes left for Germany. Returning eight months later, they began to live together as a married couple. This provoked a public outrage and George Eliot, who now called herself Mrs or Marian Lewes, bore the brunt of the hostility. Isaac firmly cut off all communication with her, only resuming it again twenty-four years later after Lewes had died (1878). Although at first only very few of George Eliot's close friends supported and visited her, eventually the success of her writing and its moral force, combined with her own personal integrity, earned her respect from many and a degree of acceptance from society. Later, although critics continued to ridicule and resent her, the social gatherings held at the Lewes's home on Sunday afternoons were attended by their friends and associates, amongst them some of the most important writers and thinkers of the period, including Charles Dickens, Henry James, Alfred Lord Tennyson, and Matthew Arnold.

During her period of virtual isolation following her return to England, George Eliot began to write fiction using her pseudonym George Eliot. Lewes was central in supporting and encouraging her, despite her almost constant lack of confidence, and in protecting her from negative reviews. Their common interest in science, philosophy and literature (Lewes wrote on all of these subjects) clearly proved stimulating to George Eliot's creative work and her wide intellectual interests inform all her writing. It seems significant that the last letter that Lewes wrote before his death from cancer was to John Blackwood, accompanying the first part of George Eliot's manuscript for her collection of essays (eventually published as *Impressions of Theophrastus Such* in 1879), thus supporting her writing to the end of his life.

George Eliot was devastated by the loss of Lewes and so great was her grief that she did not attend his funeral in Highgate Cemetery. After a few months she married a long-standing friend John Cross. Her brother sent her a letter of congratulations, but they never saw each other again.

George Eliot died eight months after her marriage in December 1880. She was refused a burial in Poet's Corner in Westminster Abbey and was buried next to Lewes. Many of the obituaries obliterated or omitted reference to her life with Lewes.

In several respects *The Mill on the Floss* can be seen to echo George Eliot's life: it is set in the period in which she was growing up and in a similar rural setting to Arbury Estate with Arbury Mill close by. The parent–child relationships seem similar and, like George Eliot, Maggie experiences a period of intense evangelical belief which she eventually renounces. Maggie's feelings of intellectual and emotional isolation within her family also seem to echo those of George Eliot. The relationship between Maggie and Tom closely resembles that between George Eliot and her brother in terms of the childhood closeness and George Eliot's adoration of Isaac, and in terms of Isaac's intense disapproval of her independence and her unconventional behaviour.

HER OTHER WORKS

George Eliot only began to write fiction in her late thirties. The majority of her novels are set in the past and are, to a certain extent, a documentation of the changing social and economic conditions of the people, places and times she depicts. Her heroes and heroines are often searching for a belief system to explain and give direction to their lives. Before and during this fiction-writing period she was well known as a critical writer and she wrote reviews, articles, commentaries and essays on a broad range of subjects which were widely published in newspapers, journals and periodicals. She also wrote short stories and poems. Her early fiction takes rural life as its context and draws imaginatively and, in some ways, biographically on George Eliot's experience of growing up in provincial Warwickshire. In fact, some of the characters in George Eliot's first novel, *Scenes of Clerical Life* (1858), were drawn so recognisably from actual people in Warwickshire that it was suspected that a local clergyman, Joseph Liggins, was the author.

Scenes of Clerical Life was actually three long stories published together in 1858. The first of these stories, 'The Sad Fortunes of the Reverend Amos Barton', was submitted by Lewes to John Blackwood, editor of *Blackwood's Edinburgh Magazine*, in November 1856 on behalf of the writer, whom he called 'my clerical friend'. It was serialised anonymously, though 'George Eliot' came into existence when she signed her letter to William Blackwood with this name in February 1857. There is some **irony** in the title of this first novel and in Lewes's reference to her given her attacks on orthodox Christian belief. However, George Eliot has often been described as a moralist and her fiction does contain a moral message, though not one based on orthodox religious teaching. Rather, she aims to arouse people's emotions and sympathies with her art as a way of guiding them to act in ways which are socially right.

Adam Bede, published in February 1859, was her second novel and it gained instant popularity and received great critical acclaim. The success of this novel, however, only added to the increasing speculation about the identity of George Eliot. Finally towards the end of 1859 news broke of her real identity, producing some severe personal criticism and prompting negative reviews of her next novel, *The Mill on the Floss* (1860). The **satirical** passages dealing with the voice of 'public opinion' in this novel could be read as an outlet for George Eliot's feelings about the pronounced double standard for men and women (especially given the harsh judgements made about her professional and personal life at this time).

Her short story, 'The Lifted Veil', was published anonymously in *Blackwood's Edinburgh Magazine* in July 1859. This was followed in 1861 by *Silas Marner* which, like her first two novels, has a rural setting. As in *The Mill on the Floss*, George Eliot explores the **Romantic** emphasis on the importance of preserving childhood memories and affections into adulthood in order to develop spiritually. In both novels children and childhood are catalysts for good deeds and have a regenerative and reforming impact. Mr Tulliver, for instance, decides not to call in his debt from his sister when he thinks of Tom and Maggie, and Silas's life is transformed when, after his money has been stolen, Eppie is abandoned on his doorstep. *Romola* (1863) is set in Renaissance Italy, and is considered to be George Eliot's most ambitious novel. Romola, like Maggie, suffers unequal treatment in terms of education, and escapes from stifling **patriarchal** constraints by water. A novella, *Brother Jacob*, was published in 1864, and *Felix Holt, The Radical* in 1866. Again set in the Midlands of the 1830s, *Felix Holt* has a strong political emphasis and an urban setting. The narrative poem, 'The Spanish Gypsy', set in fifteenth-century Spain, was published in 1868 and the poetic drama 'Armgart' in 1870.

Middlemarch, which began to be serialised in 1871, is held to be George Eliot's greatest novel and indeed one of the greatest novels in English. Set at the time of the first Reform Bill (1832) in a provincial town in the Midlands, it deals more widely than any of her other fiction with the contemporary issues and changes experienced in the nineteenth century. Electoral reform, medical advances and the resistance to these, the developments in transport, agricultural improvements, women's education, inheritance law, evangelical expansion and the theories of evolution are all embraced. In *Middlemarch* George Eliot tackles in greater depth some of the issues *The Mill on the Floss* raises, notably the restrictions on women's lives and ambitions caused by social customs and conventional ideas of romance. Finally, *Daniel Deronda* (1876) set in the mid-Victorian present, takes the possibility of finding a home for Jewish people in Europe as its central concern.

George Eliot also wrote poetry, much of which was published in various magazines from 1865 onwards. The five poems she wrote in 1869 ('Agatha', 'How Lisa Loved the King', the eleven-sonnet sequence 'Brother and Sister', 'Stradivarius' and 'The Legend of Jubal') were published together in *The Legend of Jubal, and Other Poems* in 1874, along with 'O May I Join the Choir Invisible'.

HISTORICAL BACKGROUND

MATERIAL AND POLITICAL

During the nineteenth century, Britain, and particularly England, experienced a period of unprecedented change in all aspects of life: demographic, economic, social, scientific, technological and moral. As a result of such dramatic changes human existence became more mechanised and more uncertain. The Industrial Revolution brought new kinds of machinery and steam power which led to unemployment in some areas and to massive migrations to urban areas. Cities expanded rapidly and unhealthily as a result of this massive influx, and the division between rich and poor became more exaggerated; the great gulf of understanding between the classes is summed up in Benjamin Disraeli's novel *Sibil: or, the Two Nations* (1845).

With rapid developments of the economy and of trade, the struggle for political power became central as the commercially successful middle classes vied for power with those who traditionally ruled the country – the landed aristocracy and their heirs. Those who had no political power, the labouring classes, felt increasingly disempowered as changes in employment had a detrimental effect. Political reform around the issue of parliamentary representation was a cause for much upheaval throughout the century, with the two Reform Acts of 1832 and 1867 acting as focal points. *The Mill on the Floss*, *Felix Holt* and *Middlemarch* are all set in the period of the first Reform Act. Although *The Mill on the Floss* does not engage explicitly with this issue of political reform, it does refer to the Roman Catholic Emancipation Act of 1829, passed by the Duke of Wellington (then Prime Minister), which, like the Reform Act evoked a sense of threat and uncertainty with regard to the balance of political power.

The Mill on the Floss offers two views on such changes: Mr Tulliver holds conservative views and looks back nostalgically to the past and to the tradition of his family working in harmony with nature; Mr Deane, on the other hand, embraces change and is proud of Victorian achievement. Like many other social critics and writers (among them Thomas Carlyle, John Ruskin, Matthew Arnold, Charles Dickens, William Thackeray and Elizabeth Gaskell), George Eliot objected to the intense human suffering that industrial and economic changes brought to the daily lives of millions of people. This suffering was hypocritically obscured beneath technological achievements, commercial success and the 'glories' of Empire. At the point at which Maggie adopts the religious teaching of Thomas à Kempis, the authorial voice draws attention to the function of religion in a capitalist society. She not only criticises the spiritual complacency of those living in luxury, but also assumes what we would now call a Marxist stance in highlighting the gross inequalities necessary to maintain 'good society' and the solution that religion offered to some of those in dire circumstances (pp. 385–6).

THOUGHT AND BELIEF

In *The Mill on the Floss* George Eliot documents a typically provincial perception of religion as being more concerned with hereditary and social custom than with Christian spirituality or morality. Dr Kenn's disillusionment with the superficiality of belief in St Ogg's highlights this and George Eliot **ironically** shows that religion is seen merely as a means to an end: Mr Stelling sees preaching as another way to achieve his social and personal ambitions (p. 203), and Tom sees his prayers as a means of achieving success in remembering his Latin (p. 211). However, Anglican complacency was shaken by the reforming zeal of the evangelical Christian movement. Although George Eliot abandoned her evangelical belief, her experience of evangelism continued to have an effect and this is seen in Maggie's strong sense of duty and other characters' self-examinations of their motivation.

Like many other intellectuals, George Eliot herself moved towards a position of philosophic agnosticism. She sought a moral order and ethical guidance outside Christian doctrine, and the great changes in perception and conceptualisation of spirituality and society aided the formation of her ideas. Traditional Christianity was challenged by German intellectuals who sought to unravel biblical history from its mythical elements. George Eliot's own translations of David Strauss's *Life of Jesus* (1846) and Ludwig Feuerbach's *Essence of Christianity* (1854) were central in the challenge to orthodox Christianity. George Eliot's thought and writing were affected by Ludwig Feuerbach's **humanism**, his central theory that God was an imaginary product of humankind's projection of human qualities and ideals, and his criticism of Christianity's failure to recognise and tolerate individual difference. In her narrative style, her creation of characters and her thematic structuring, George Eliot made a case for tolerance and sympathy, and the narrator in *The Mill on the Floss* concurs with a Feuerbachian idea that in matters of moral judgement there is 'no master key that will fit all cases' and no 'ready-made patent method' (p. 628). Ludwig Feuerbach's discussion of sexuality as part of his analysis of morality, love and imagination offered George Eliot a theoretical basis for her own conception of the power and moral importance of sexual desire and sensuality.

Established religious certainties were also challenged by scientific discovery and thought. George Eliot was still writing *The Mill on the Floss* when Charles Darwin's *On the Origin of Species by Natural Selection, or The Preservation of Favoured Races in the Struggle for Life* was published in 1859. However, the ideas that it propounded were ideas with which George Eliot was familiar and which were already being expressed in fiction. Ideas of evolution had been slowly emerging in the work of biologists and geologists throughout the century, ideas which collided violently with Christian notions of origin and the acceptance of the Bible as a historical record. Charles Lyell's *Principles of Geology* (1830) began the doubts about the rapid creation of the earth, and Robert Chambers's *Vestiges of the Natural History of Creation* (1844) offered a theory of human evolution from lower forms of life (see Gillian Beer's *Darwin's Plots: Evolutionary Narrative in Darwin, George Eliot and Nineteenth-Century Fiction*, Ark Paperbacks, 1983, for an illuminating discussion of these matters).

Lewes and George Eliot saw Charles Darwin's theory of evolution as a culmination of many gradualist theories of development in the natural sciences, running parallel with which was the development of theories of social evolution. The theories of the German sociologist, Wilhelm Heinrich von Riehl, the French philosopher, Auguste Comte, the English social theorist and George Eliot's close friend, Herbert Spencer, and the writings of George Henry Lewes all contributed to George Eliot's ideas about social evolution. In these theories society was perceived as evolving like a biological organism, and it was assumed that the close connection between the elements of the organism (society) in terms of past and present social bonds would give rise to a **humanistic** moral system. George Eliot's description of the slow evolution of St Ogg's indicates the influence of this theory of social development, and the moral scheme of the novel draws on the moral dimension of this scientific approach.

Evolutionary theories, then, with their emphasis on kinship, environment and gradual change throughout time, offered a basis for arguing for social improvements and helped George Eliot to formulate a sense of morality that did not rely on Christian teaching. Like Charles Darwin's *On the Origin of Species*, *The Mill on the Floss* is concerned with origins, with kinship and heredity, with the influence of environment, with the interconnection of characters' lives and with the crucial continuum of past, present and future. In the creation of Maggie's central dilemma, which is that she is torn between following her instinctive, sensual and animal instincts and adhering to her sense of social duty and responsibility, George Eliot seems to diverge from Darwinian theory. However, the issues of human conscience and moral sense that George Eliot raises in her novel come to the fore in Charles Darwin's later work, *The Descent of Man* (1871). In his theorising about sexual selection, Charles Darwin claimed that women's powers of intellect, imagination and manual dexterity were inferior to those of men and that, unlike other species, in humans it was the male who was more able to choose a sexual partner. George Eliot clearly anticipated and refuted such ideas in *The Mill on the Floss* where not only is Maggie emotionally, morally and intellectually Tom's superior, but the perception of women's inferiority is what underlies Maggie's tragedy.

THE WOMAN QUESTION

George Eliot's position over the 'Woman Question' which dominated the Victorian period is ambivalent. This 'Question' involved debate over the unequal social, political, economic and legal position of women. Women's roles in the private and public sphere, educational and employment rights and opportunities, and women's suffrage were some of the key focal points, as were more general issues about morality, sexuality and self-fulfilment. Although many of George Eliot's close female friends were actively involved with the Victorian Women's Movement, George Eliot did not give it her public support. She did, however, follow the developments and debates and gave some financial support to the movement for women's education.

George Eliot agreed with Lewes that women have something different to contribute to literary expression, namely an emotional dimension. However, George Eliot's position is complex: she criticised 'lady novelists' for being too emotional and chose to assume not only a male pseudonym, but also a male narrative voice. Although in *The Mill on The Floss* George Eliot argues against the illogicality of social conventions which deny Maggie the education she is capable of and ridicules the superficial aspects of feminine identity, Maggie is depicted as being emotionally volatile and vulnerable. It is unclear whether George Eliot considers Maggie's psychological identity to be a result of her powerless position in society (a **constructionist** view) or an innate aspect of her female biology (an **essentialist** view). What is clear is that she did not allow her most autobiographical heroine to achieve the success that she herself did. As feminist critics suggest, George Eliot's perspective on **feminism** is contradictory (see Critical History and Broader Perspectives – Contemporary Approaches).

L<small>ITERARY</small> BACKGROUND

In her writing, George Eliot expresses a complex combination of intellect, insight and intuition and the influence of the **Romantic** precursors is evident, as it is with many other Victorian writers. The tension between Romantic impulses (involving the imagination, feelings, sensual and sexual desires, and the power and spirituality of nature) and representations of ordinary, quotidian life forms a constant dynamic in George Eliot's writing. Sir Walter Scott and William Wordsworth were especially significant influences. Like Sir Walter Scott, particularly in his *Waverley* novels, George Eliot in *The Mill on the Floss* fuses the historical and realistic modes of writing with the Romantic. Like Sir Walter Scott, she offers psychological insight, considering the effect of childhood and education on the development of her characters and on subsequent history. Like William Wordsworth, she considers the lives of ordinary individuals, echoing his aim in writing the *Lyrical Ballads*, which was 'to make the incidents of common life interesting by tracing in them, truly not ostentatiously, the primary laws of our nature' (1800 Preface to *Lyrical Ballads*, by William Wordsworth, and Samuel Taylor Coleridge, R.L. Brett and A.R. Jones, eds., Methuen, 1963, p. 244–5). However, George Eliot's portayal of ordinary lives produced a mixed response from her critics. Some, like John Ruskin, disparaged her depiction of 'the blotches, burrs and pimples' of everyday life in *The Mill on the Floss* (in David Carroll, ed., *George Eliot: The Critical Heritage*, Routledge and Kegan Paul, 1971, p. 167).

In *The Mill on the Floss* George Eliot was also clearly influenced by the Romantic fascination with the child and with childhood. The

Romantic poets, especially William Blake and William Wordsworth, refuted eighteenth-century ideas about children's minds and personalities being a blank page on to which social and moral principles need to be imprinted (as the philosopher John Locke, suggests). Instead, following the ideas of the French Philosopher, Jean Jacques Rousseau, they offered a revaluation of childhood, claiming that children have intuitive insight and wisdom which is lost in adulthood. In particular William Wordsworth's understanding of childhood as a crucial time for the development of the inner self seems especially significant to the development of Maggie. The influence of childhood is important for other characters too. For instance, when Mr Tulliver is struggling to decide whether or not to work for Wakem, his memories of his own childhood not only explain his strong attachment to Dorlcote Mill, but win sympathy from the reader.

Like some of her contemporaries, George Eliot breaks away from conventionally didactic or sentimental depictions of children. George Eliot's Tom and Maggie are psychologically complex, like Charlotte Brontë's Jane Eyre, and she captures the often fraught emotions of childhood and early adolescence. Unlike Charlotte Brontë's and Charles Dickens's depiction of lonely and orphaned children, however, Maggie and Tom have a comfortable home, a close relationship with one of their parents, and a close relationship with each other.

George Eliot also read and admired the work of her contemporaries, amongst them Elizabeth Gaskell, William Thackeray and Charlotte Brontë. In particular she admired the way that Elizabeth Gaskell's writing sought to raise awareness of, and gain sympathy for, the plight of ordinary working people, and praised Charles Dickens's intention of extending the reader's sympathy, although her own writing differed from his more stylised, rhetorical and melodramatic expression. European writers, such as Johann Wolfgang von Goethe, Honoré de Balzac and George Sand also influenced her writing.

PART SIX

CRITICAL HISTORY AND BROADER PERSPECTIVES

RECEPTION AND EARLY REVIEWS

Throughout her fiction-writing career George Eliot received a great deal of attention from critics. *The Mill on the Floss* provoked a mixed response and divided her readers. Critics praised her depiction of childhood for its authenticity and for its moral teaching. However, some critics were disappointed and regretted the loss of the rural charm she evoked in *Adam Bede*. Instead they saw the characters in *The Mill on the Floss* as being 'prosaic, selfish, nasty', with lives of 'sordid ... vulgar respectability'; the Dodsons were especially criticised as being 'stingy, selfish wretches' (E.S. Dallas, *The Times* (1860), in David Carroll, ed., *George Eliot: The Critical Heritage*, Routledge and Kegan Paul, 1971, pp. 132, 133, 135). The most vehement criticism was levelled at the third volume of the novel: Maggie's conflict between desire and duty was felt to be inconsistent with the development of the first two volumes, and her 'overmastering passion' and unlikely choice of lover were the focus of several negative comments (unsigned reviews in the *Saturday Review* (1860), and *Dublin University Magazine* (1861), in Carroll, p. 119). David Carroll, in his introduction to *George Eliot: The Critical Heritage*, claims that the real problem for the critics was that George Eliot put their sense of morality to the test.

The revelation of George Eliot's real identity led to a change in tone of some criticism; since Victorian readers read literature for its truthfulness to reality and for moral edification, the contradiction between George Eliot's social position and the moral stance taken in her fiction caused critics to feel deceived. The revelation also led to a change in the focus of several critics. Her novels were interpreted in terms of the intellectual and philosophical views she put forward in the *Westminster Review* and, as a result, she became elevated as a 'sage' and separated from her contemporary fiction writers (see John Holloway's *The Victorian Sage*, 1953). Her scandalous personal life also led to an emphasis on the sexual misconduct in her novels. A common criticism in the early and later considerations of *The Mill on the Floss* is the ending, because it does not allow Maggie to act on her moral decision, and marks an abrupt break with the **realism** of the novel. Despite this negative criticism, however, the novel soon became popular.

David Carroll, *George Eliot: The Critical Heritage*, Routledge and Kegan Paul, 1971
> Contains a good range of early reviews and criticism

Gordon S. Haight, ed., *A Century of George Eliot Criticism*, Methuen and Co., 1966 (first published Houghton Mifflin Company, 1965)
> Contains a wide range of reviews and critical essays from the mid nineteenth to the mid twentieth century

CRITICAL HISTORY

Her early critics also experienced a sense of contradiction between George Eliot's female identity and the 'masculine' intellect demonstrated in her novels. As Deidre David notes, 'Eliot found her work constantly evaluated in terms of its fidelity (or not) to "female" or "feminine" qualities. She is praised and blamed for writing like a woman – and for writing like a man' (*Intellectual Women and Victorian Patriarchy*, Macmillan, 1987, p. 165). In *George Eliot* (Macmillan, 1902), Leslie Stephen describes her as a 'pre-eminently feminine' writer and argues that her literary and intellectual achievement was limited because she was a woman. He claims that her inadequacy is exposed in her creation of male characters, for instance: 'George Eliot did not herself understand what a mere hair-dresser's block she was describing in Mr Stephen Guest' (p. 104).

George Eliot's reputation began to decline rapidly immediately after her death in 1880, possibly in part owing to John Cross's biography of her, *George Eliot's Life, as Related in her Letters and Journals* (1885). This created a gloomy moralistic impression of her which then transferred to her novels. In the climate of **modernist** experiment in the early years of the twentieth century, the realist form and didactic moralism of George Eliot's writing was severely criticised. In *Early Victorian Novelists* (1935) David Cecil continued this criticism, but, taking a **formalist** approach in his criticism, he did consider George Eliot to be the first modern novelist because she constructed a novel around an idea.

Virginia Woolf's voice is one exception to the prevailing views of George Eliot and her art in the early twentieth century. Writing from a **feminist** perspective, Virginia Woolf reassesses George Eliot, paving the way for later feminist re-evaluations of George Eliot and her work. She asserts that George Eliot 'would not renounce her own inheritance – the difference of view, the different standard', and identifies George Eliot's heroines as a source of difficulty, especially for male critics, because they express the unfulfilled ambitions and needs of women in Victorian **patriarchal** society ('George Eliot', the *Times Literary Supplement*, 1919, in Haight, p. 189).

F. R. Leavis (in *The Great Tradition: George Eliot, Henry James, and Joseph Conrad*, 1948) was the first major critic to object to Henry James's influential assessments of George Eliot's literary practice. Instead of viewing aesthetic and formal qualities as separate from moral concerns (as Henry James did), F.R. Leavis saw form and morals as inextricably connected. He was influenced by the **formalist** approach of the American **New Critics**, who asserted the centrality of the close reading of texts and the autonomy of literature. A weakness he sees in *The Mill on the Floss* is George Eliot's emotional involvement with Maggie and her self-idealisation through the character. He also criticises the ending as immature.

Further critical assessments of George Eliot in the 1950s and 1960s also took a formalist approach. Barbara Hardy, in *The Novels of George Eliot: A Study in Form* (1959), argued that form or thematic structure is not in opposition to the realistic, moral and philosophical aspects of George Eliot's work. Rather, form controls these aspects. For example, even though George Eliot's characters have an irrevocable destiny, Barbara Hardy argues that thematic patterning and form also suggest alternative destinies which her characters could choose. In *The Mill on the Floss* it is the river imagery that conveys the possibility of an alternative destiny for Maggie. The fact that the choice is repeated, as is Maggie's decision not to follow this alternative destiny, means that the moral purpose of the novel has been reiterated and strengthened by the thematic structuring and use of repetition.

Other critics challenge views such as Barbara Hardy's and argue that form and pattern did not reconcile George Eliot's moral purpose with realistic representation. These critics also focus on the problem that language presents for realistic representation, since language is not mimetic, transparent or value-free. Critical theories that incorporate such a perspective on language include **Marxist, feminist** and **deconstructionist** theories. Early Marxist critics analyse the depiction of social and economic conditions, the relationships between the classes, and how far the values inherent in texts endorse and/or criticise dominant bourgeois ideology. Raymond Williams is a key figure in developing Marxist literary criticism. He argues that George Eliot's attempt to create a rural community is compromised by her 'nineteenth-century middle-class imagination'. Terry Eagleton also explores the difficulties of reconciling **realism** and ideology in George Eliot's writing and he looks to how ideology is reflected and produced in novels. Later Marxist criticism has been influenced by **structuralism** and **post-structuralism**, and in the last twenty years language has been a major critical focus for discussion of George Eliot's writing.

Taking a post-structuralist approach, Colin MacCabe argues that George Eliot's texts create a **hierarchy of discourses** in which the narrator's voice is privileged and claim to reflect reality like a mirror. He argues that this is a typical feature of the **classic realist text**. Deconstructionist critics, such as the American J. Hillis Miller, go further than this and argue that George Eliot deconstructs the classic realist text even as she apparently writes it. Jonathan Arac similarly argues that George Eliot was controlling the deconstruction of realism in *The Mill on the Floss*. Feminist criticism has taken a great interest in *The Mill on the Floss*. The novel's focus on the **patriarchal** social restrictions on the emotional, psychological and social development of a young woman, its revision of the masculine genre of the **Bildungsroman**, and its autobiographical aspects offer fruitful opportunities for the discussion of the experience of a woman in a male-dominated culture. Elaine Showalter's *A Literature of Their Own: From Charlotte Brontë to Doris Lessing* (1977), presents a challenge to F.R. Leavis's 'Great Traditionalism', and, establishing a tradition of women's writing, relocates George Eliot in the context of other women writers. Early feminist critics analyse the images of women, genre, themes, imagery and structures in women's writing. Later feminist critics are influenced by other critical approaches, such as those of **psychoanalytic criticism** and post-structuralism. In Sandra Gilbert and Susan Gubar's interpretations, for instance, the influence of psychoanalytic interpretation is clear, and other critics have read George Eliot's fiction in the light of Freudian and Lacanian theory (Dianne F. Sadoff, for example). The opening dream and the non-realistic ending, plus the 'family romance' which is played out in this novel all give scope for psychoanalytical readings.

Terry Eagleton, *Criticism and Ideology: A Study in Marxist Literary Theory*, New Left Books, 1976

Barbara Hardy, in *The Novels of George Eliot: A Study in Form*, the Athlone Press, 1963, first published 1959

Barbara Hardy, ed., *Critical Essays on George Eliot*, Routledge and Kegan Paul, 1970
> Contains an essay on *The Mill on the Floss* by Barbara Hardy which compares it to Charles Dickens's *David Copperfield* and Charlotte Brontë's *Jane Eyre*

F.R. Leavis, *The Great Tradition: George Eliot, Henry James, and Joseph Conrad*, Chatto and Windus, 1948
> A pioneering reappraisal of George Eliot's art

Colin MacCabe, 'The End of a Metalanguage: From George Eliot to *Dubliners*', in his book *James Joyce and the Revolution of the Word*, Macmillan Press, 1978. Reprinted in K.M. Newton, *George Eliot*

K.M. Newton, ed., *George Eliot*, Longman, 1991
> Introduction contains a comprehensive discussion of contemporary critical approaches to George Eliot

Dianne F. Sadoff, *Monsters of Affection: Dickens, Eliot and Brontë on Fatherhood*, Johns Hopkins University Press, 1982
> Draws on Freudian theories and the idea of paternal seduction

Elaine Showalter, *A Literature of Their Own: From Charlotte Brontë to Doris Lessing*, Virago Press Ltd., 1978, first published, 1977
> Identifies a developing tradition of women's writing in the nineteenth and twentieth centuries; Elaine Showalter discusses this development in terms of feminine, female, and feminist stages

Raymond Williams, *The English Novel From Dickens to Lawrence*, Chatto and Windus, 1971
> Useful analysis of how George Eliot's plots, depiction of working-class characters, and address to the reader can be seen to reflect bourgeois values

FEMINIST CRITICISMS

Feminist criticisms largely debate how far George Eliot's writing can be read as sympathetic to feminism. George Eliot and her novels are seen as offering ambiguous and contradictory opportunities for feminist interpretation, and most feminist critics argue that her writing is both critical of and complicit with dominant **patriarchal** ideologies concerning gender identity, roles and social positions.

George Eliot's assumption of a male pseudonym (although ostensibly for the pragmatic reason of not wanting her work to be prejudged as inferior because written by a woman) has been taken as a starting point for theorising about her attitude to women and feminism, her role as a writer, and her identity as a woman. In *George Eliot*, Kristin Brady suggests a range of theories about George Eliot's use of a male pseudonym, from Elaine Showalter's idea that George Eliot sought to avoid patriarchal judgements, to Mary Jacobus's explanation that the male name expresses George Eliot's self-hatred and her ambivalent attitude towards her role as a woman writer (Brady, p. 48). Her retention of the name George Eliot for her fictional writing, even when her identity was discovered, has been interpreted as a feminist strategy which confounds gendered categories of 'male author' or 'lady novelist' (Brady, p. 50).

Feminist critics in the 1970s were quite hostile to George Eliot and the plots she creates for her heroines because they are not permitted to fulfil their intellectual ambitions or follow their sexual desires. Discussing George Eliot's representation of Maggie, Elaine Showalter states that she 'analyses sympathetically the unfulfilled longings of an intelligent young woman in a narrow and oppressive society, but nonetheless elevates suffering into a female career' (p. 125). She reads Maggie as largely complicit with dominant cultural conceptions of womanhood and femininity: 'Maggie is the progenitor of a heroine who identifies passivity and renunciation with womanhood, who finds it easier, more natural, and in a mystical way more satisfying, to destroy herself than to live in a world without opium or fantasy, where she must fight to survive' (p. 131).

Sandra Gilbert and Susan Gubar argue that George Eliot's punishment of her heroines is an endorsement of the Victorian ideal of feminine self-renunciation. They see this, plus her disparaging remarks about other women writers and her assumption of a male pseudonym, as suggesting 'the depth of her need to evade identification with her own sex' and her 'internalisation of patriarchal culture's definition of the woman as the "other"' (p. 466). They argue that the contradictions that George Eliot embodies are resolved through her committing 'acts of vengeance against her own characters' (p. 479). Although she 'saves' her female characters from explicitly expressing their rage at their repression, they are implicated in the author's violence in her destruction of characters. This is clearly seen in *The Mill on the Floss* where Maggie ostensibly tries to save Tom, but in fact helps the author to destroy this symbol of oppressive patriarchal power. Sandra Gilbert and Susan Gubar sum up their interpretation of this ending:

> The brother who has oppressed her by taking first place in their parents' esteem, by sneering at her intellectual ambition, by curtailing her freedom to live or even imagine her own life, and by condemning her harshly in the light of his restrictive moral standards is finally punished when she goes to 'save' him from the rising tides only to drag him down into the dark deep in her 'embrace' of death (p. 494)

They discuss the fraught relationship of Maggie and Tom in terms of the larger tensions between the forces of culture (associated with male power and industry) and nature (associated with female emotion and reproduction), and explore Maggie's entrapment in the double bind in which **patriarchal** culture places women. She is dependent on men for success, but is prevented from achieving a relationship with a man, which would enable this success, because of her father's feud with Wakem and because of Tom's disapproval of her relationship with Stephen. Her sympathetic identification with Lucy, they argue, does offer the possibility of a break from complete isolation, and is an example of the 'heroism of sisterhood within patriarchy' found in George Eliot's writing (p. 518).

Other feminist critics, such as Deidre David and J.R. Perkin, have argued that Sandra Gilbert and Susan Gubar's reading cuts George Eliot off from her historical and political context. By contrast, Gillian Beer's *George Eliot* (1986) offers a historically-based defence of George Eliot's writing and practice. Highlighting George Eliot's connections with other prominent feminists, Gillian Beer stresses the author's **feminist** commitment and her courage. She questions Sandra Gilbert and Susan Gubar's views on George Eliot's endorsement of renunciation, and argues that balancing renunciation and resistance is at the centre of the major dramatic encounters in George Eliot's novels. Instead of focusing primarily on the representations of women in George Eliot's writing, Gillian Beer considers the male–female relationships and George Eliot's representation of men and masculinity as a sign of her scope as a writer. She argues that for George Eliot, 'Writing as a woman must mean writing as a human', and that George Eliot looks for connections as well as differences between men and women. So for instance, Gillian Beer considers that Tom also suffers from his experiences as a male: his education stifles him and his assumption of the manly role induces him to behave in a stubborn and arrogant manner.

More recent criticisms focus on a duality in the narrative structure or plotting. Kristen Brady discusses *The Mill on the Floss* in terms of a double plot: a realistic or historical plot and what she calls 'the gender plot' (p. 129). The realistic plot is associated with the male-dominated literary mainstream, with the masculine power structure, and with social and narrative **determinism**; the gender plot, on the other hand, comes into play when heroines are in danger of being swamped by **patriarchal** conventions. The genre is changed to accommodate the female gender. The flood at the end of the novel, she argues, is not George Eliot's escape from too complex a plot, but rather the gender plot moving the action 'into a realm outside patriarchy' (p. 129).

The final words that George Eliot is known to have written are 'a sister's affection', but George Eliot continues to be, in Gillian Beer's words, 'a knot of controversy for feminist critics', and not easily a **feminist** 'sister' at all (p. 3).

Gillian Beer, *George Eliot*, Indiana University Press, 1986

> A comprehensive discussion of George Eliot's work and life, with a chapter on *The Mill on the Floss*

Kristen Brady, *George Eliot*, Macmillan Education Ltd., 1992

> An accessible discussion of George Eliot's life and writing from a feminist perspective, with a chapter on *The Mill on the Floss*

Deidre David, *Intellectual Women and Victorian Patriarchy*, Macmillan Press, 1987

Discussion of George Eliot as an intellectual woman, and as a critic of and an accomplice with patriarchal ideologies

Sandra Gilbert and Susan Gubar, *The Mad Woman in the Attic: The Woman Writer and the Nineteenth-Century Literary Imagination*, Yale University Press, 1979

Elaine Showalter A Literature of Their Own: From Charlotte Brontë to Doris Lessing, Virago Press Ltd, 1978, first published 1997.

DECONSTRUCTIONIST APPROACHES

Post-structuralist approaches emphasise the doubleness and indeterminacy of meaning, drawing attention to the contradictions and ambiguities in George Eliot's writing. Jonathan Arac addresses the complexity and instability of the meaning and narrative structure in *The Mill on the Floss*. In demonstrating George Eliot's awareness that language is duplicitous, metaphorical and hyperbolic, he shows that her novel is not naively realistic. He begins with a harmonious reading of the novel, moving from the unity of 'Boy and Girl', through the alienation of 'Downfall', to the reunion of 'Final Rescue', but reveals that the return to unity is 'specious and spurious' and merely highlights the divisions that have existed all along (see Arac in K.M. Newton, ed., George Eliot, p. 67). He suggests that at one level the patterns of harmony and completeness are assured by science (especially with reference to evolution and to ideas of human origin and interrelation with the natural world), and by reference to the past and childhood via memory. However, he shows how the realistic aspects of the novel are disrupted by the excessive **romantic** elements, which he calls a 'hyperbolic' pattern. This second pattern of 'romantic excess' contrasts with the ordered realistic pattern and demonstrates George Eliot's **deconstruction** of the **realist** text she is writing. He concludes by saying that George Eliot's awareness that language can never exactly coincide with reality is 'realistic in its attempt to unsettle cultural complacencies' (see Newton, p. 80).

Mary Jacobus engages with post-structuralist concerns about language from a **feminist** perspective. She argues that women are subordinated by dominant linguistic and cultural discourses because women are located as 'other', as the negative and inferior term in the system of **binary opposites** which operates in thought and language. These oppositions are disrupted in *The Mill on the Floss* through Maggie's understanding and use of Latin (a male-dominated discourse from which women were traditionally excluded because a classical education was denied them). The fact that Maggie knows that women spoke Latin in the past and that she has taught herself Latin undermines women's exclusion from this discourse. Further, Maggie's awareness that language has multiple meanings, whereby 'bonus' can mean 'good' and 'gift', alerts us to George Eliot's awareness that linguistic meaning is unstable and discourses not as fixed as they may seem. In this way dominant discourses are undermined and deconstructed.

Jonathan Arac, 'Rhetoric and Realism in Nineteenth-Century Fiction: Hyperbole in *The Mill on The Floss*', 1979, in K.M. Newton, ed., *George Eliot*, Longman, 1991

Mary Jacobus, 'Men of Maxims and *The Mill on the Floss*', 1986, in K.M. Newton, ed., *George Eliot*, Longman, 1991

CHRONOLOGY

World events		George Eliot	Literature & science
	1857	Marian Evans first uses the name 'George Eliot'	Charles Dickens, *Little Dorrit* Gustave Flaubert, *Madame Bovary* Anthony Trollope, *Barchester Towers* Charles Baudelaire, *Les Fleurs du Mal*
	1858	Publication of *Scenes of Clerical Life*, George Eliot's first novel	First transatlantic cable is laid Charles Darwin and Alfred Wallace present papers to the Linnaen Society on the subject of evolution
	1859	*Adam Bede* 'The Lifted Veil' (in *Blackwood's Edinburgh Magazine*) News breaks of George Eliot's real identity	Charles Darwin, *On the Origin of Species by Means of Natural Selection* Charles Dickens, *A Tale of Two Cities*
Unification of Italy	**1860**	***Mill on the Floss*** published	Wilkie Collins, *The Woman in White* Joseph Swan invents the electric lamp
American Civil War begins Albert, the Prince Consort dies	**1861**	*Silas Marner* published	Charles Dickens, *Great Expectations*

World events		George Eliot	Literature & science
Revised Code' introduces government grants for schools; these are dependent on the pupils' progress in 'the three Rs'	1862	*Romola* serialised in the Cornhill Magazine	International Exhibition of Industry and Science opens in London Victor Hugo, *Les Miserables*
	1863	*Romola* published	Charles Kingsley, *The Water Babies*
	1864	*Brother Jacob*, a novella, published	Public debate on Darwinian theory of evolution in Oxford. Benjamin Disraeli declares that he is 'on the side of the angels' Joseph Swan patents a driving chain for the textile industry; it is later developed for use in bicycles
American Civil War ends William Booth leads the first of his evangelical Christian Mission meetings in London; later renamed the Salvation Army	1865		Lewis Carroll, *Alice's Adventures in Wonderland* Charles Dickens, *Our Mutual Friend* Matthew Arnold, *Essays in Criticism*, first series
	1866	*Felix Holt, The Radical* published	Dostoevsky, *Crime and Punishment*

alliteration a sequence of repeated consonantal sounds in a piece of language. The matching consonants are usually at the beginning of words or stressed syllables. Alliteration is one of the most easily identifiable figures of speech and is common in poetry and prose, although it may be less immediately obvious in prose

allusion a passing reference in a work of literature to something outside itself. A writer may allude to legends, historical facts or personages, to other works of literature, or even to autobiographical details. Literary allusion describes the inclusion of passages or phrases from other literary texts, or the imitation or parody of another writer's style in order to introduce implicit contrasts or comparisons

Bildungsroman a novel that describes the protagonist's development from childhood to maturity. This development usually involves a spiritual crisis, and tends to focus on the relationship between experience, education, character and identity

binary opposition the fundamental contrasts (such as in/out, off/on, good/bad) used in structuralist methods of linguistic analysis, and in criticism, anthropology and feminism. It has been argued that binarism is fundamental to all learning and interpretation of experience, and that all processes of understanding involve discrimination and choice between opposed possibilities. Feminists point out that the lists of binary oppositions (such as active/passive, head/heart, reason/feeling, strength/ weakness) often coincide with the male/female opposition, with the masculine side of the opposition having more intrinsic value in male-dominated societies

character double Victorian novels often contain characters who seem to be doubles for each other. Usually it is a main character who is 'doubled' by one or more minor characters. The double, or alter-ego, represents what it would be inappropriate for the main character to express; the double acts out the repressed wishes or unacknowledged desires of the main character

classic realist text a text that creates the illusion that it reflects real life and experience by its selection of subject matter and its way of representing that subject matter. The major theme of the classic realist text is subjectivity, and insight into character and psychological processes are central. This presentation of fiction as if it were true has been attacked by structural critics as a trick played on the reader; they disparagingly call this 'illusionism'. They attack the hierarchy of discourses by which the author dominates the narrative and disallows a plural reading. They also attack the movement towards closure (the impression of completeness and finality achieved by the ending of some literary works, a reinstatement of order after disruption), the apparent and false completion of meaning. Fundamentally, structuralist, Marxist and post-structuralist critics attack the endorsement of bourgeois ideological values that this literary form embodies

constructionism a belief that identity is constructed, defined and developed as a result of historical, ideological, and social forces and institutions. It is the opposite of an essentialist view and denies the existence of any essential or natural qualities

deconstruction, deconstructive criticism a blanket term for certain radical critical theories which revise and develop structuralism. Many of its ideas originate in the post-structuralist linguistic philosophy developed by Jacques Derrida and it has had a strong influence on literary and critical theory. It is premised on the idea that meaning is not inherent in words, but depends on relationships between words within the system of language. It claims that all writing is intertextual and 'already written', and therefore it is not free from the effects of factors such as race, gender, class and literary institutions in its generation of meaning. Deconstruction playfully challenges traditional approaches to criticism: it offers an alternative method of analysing texts which assumes that neither language nor literary texts have stable or fixed meanings. In deconstructive readings meanings are multiple and contradiction, ambiguity and wordplay are key elements of interpretation

determinism the philosophical doctrine that all events, including human actions, are fully determined by preceding events, and so freedom of choice is illusory. Taking this approach, we perceive that narrative structures determine how plots will develop and what the characters will do; social structures determine how men and women behave

essentialism a belief that objects have a real, true essence, and intrinsic and fixed properties without which they would cease to be the same thing. When such beliefs are transferred to men and women, the eternal and immutable qualities of maleness and femaleness, feminists argue, limit and reduce women to a biological definition

feminism broadly speaking, a political movement claiming political power and economic equality of women with men. Feminist criticism and scholarship seek to explore and expose the masculine bias in texts and to challenge stereotypical representations of women in literature, as well as to 'recover' the many women writers and texts ignored by the male-biased canon. Since the late 1960s feminist theories about literature and language, and feminist interpretations of texts, have multiplied enormously and now there is an extensive range of feminist approaches which engage productively with many other theoretical approaches

foreshadow to suggest in advance what will happen later in the novel

formalism although the Formalist movement was a short-lived literary movement starting in Russia in about 1917, the formalist approach to literary criticism has become influential in its connection with structuralism. Formalist criticism concentrates on form, style and technique to the exclusion of other considerations such as social, political or philosophical aspects; its principle tenet is that the language of literature is different from ordinary language, and that the critic's task is to define this 'literariness'. It is an approach to interpretation of literary texts which has much in common with the American New Critics

hierarchy of discourses there are several layers of understanding in a text: the characters will usually only have a limited understanding of events, other characters and even themselves, whereas an omniscient narrator will have an understanding of all events and characters. At the apex of this pyramid of understanding (or hierarchy of discourses) is the author, the ultimate creator and producer of the text who controls all characters (including the narrator) and the reader's response to them. It is the author who ultimately establishes the truth of the text. The hierarchy of discourses is held to be the distinguishing feature of the classic realist text

humanism the word 'humanist' originally referred to a scholar of the humanities, especially Classical literature. During the Renaissance in the sixteenth century, European intellectuals devoted themselves to a rediscovery and intense study of Roman and Greek literature and culture. A new philosophy and view of humanity emerged; in the nineteenth century this trend in Renaissance thought was labelled 'humanism'. Reason, balance and a proper dignity for human beings were the central ideals of humanist thought. The humanists' attitude to the world is anthropocentric: instead of regarding humans as fallen, corrupt and sinful creatures, their idea of truth and excellence is based on human values and human experience.

'Humanism' in a general sense has been revived at various times since the Renaissance. The domination of society by science and industry during the nineteenth century led many writers to stress humanist values in an attempt to define a properly rounded education as a counter to the cultural aridity they saw spreading around them. Nowadays 'humanism' refers vaguely to moral philosophies which reject the supernatural beliefs of religion: many twentieth-century 'humanists', in this loose sense, are actively opposed to Christianity

irony consists of saying one thing and meaning another; it is ironic when the implicit meaning of what is said differs from the surface or apparent meaning. Irony is generated when there is an incongruity between what is expected or assumed and what is actually the case, or what seems to be the case. George Eliot often uses it as a means of criticising a character's actions or pointing out hypocrisy

Marxist criticism criticism that considers literature in relation to its capacity to reflect the struggle between the classes, and economic conditions which, according to Karl Marx (1818–83) and Friedrich Engels (1820–95), are the basis of man's intellectual and social evolution. This criticism explores the relationship between the novel and the social, political and economic conditions in which it was produced; the relationship between realism and ideology is central to such analysis

modernism is the label attached to the early twentieth-century literary movement which was typified by experimentation with literary techniques and form. This experimentation is said to be both a response to the condition of living in the modern world characterised by scientific, industrial and technological change, and a rejection of the literary conventions inherited from the nineteenth century

new criticism a name applied to a major critical movement of the 1930s and 1940s in America. The autonomy of literature is a vital tenet of this critical approach. A poem must be studied as a poem, not for any other reason (e.g. not as a piece of biographical, historical, or sociological writing). Close reading of texts is considered to be the only legitimate critical procedure

omniscient narrator a narrator is another character whom the author has created to tell the story. An omniscient narrator is one who is all seeing and all knowing (god-like, seeing every event and knowing the innermost thoughts and motives of the characters). The story can either be told using first-person narration (the narrator is a participant involved in the story, and speaks using 'I'), or using third-person narration (the narrator is outside the story and looks in on the characters referring to them as 'he', 'she', 'they'). George Eliot's narrator is also intrusive and not only reports on the characters using third-person narration, but freely adds his personal comments, speaking as 'I'

patriarchy a social and political system organised so as to give power and prestige to men, and likely to be regarded by men as the natural order of things. A term frequently used in feminist criticism

post-structuralism builds on and refines structuralism. Deconstruction is a significant post-structuralist development

psychoanalytic criticism drawing on Freud's theories of psychoanalysis (which themselves referred heavily to literature and the creative process for illustration and demonstration), psychoanalytic criticism analyses literature according to theories of the mind. More recently Jacques Lacan has reworked Freud's psychological theories in terms of structuralism, arguing that the mind is organised around a system of differences, like a language

realism a term used in two main ways: to describe the trend in nineteenth-century literature, especially in prose fiction, which aimed at presenting new truths about people in society in a non-ideal or non-romantic way; to describe a way of representing real life in literature, which is associated with this historical period

rhetorical question a question asked not for the sake of enquiry, but for emphasis: the writer or speaker expects the reader or audience to be totally convinced about the appropriate reply

Romantic in a popular sense, this term means 'to do with love', especially idealised, glamorised and facile love. It is mostly used in this Note to refer to George Eliot's incorporation of the thought and ideals which, although they occurred before the 'Romantic period' (from about 1789 to about 1830) and lasted beyond this historical time, are associated with it. Romantic attributes and interests are: (i) a concern to value feeling and emotion rather than the human capacity to reason. Logical thought and understanding are abandoned in favour of instinctive and immediate feeling or intuition. (ii) This concern with feeling leads to some of the topics typical of so-called romantic literature: natural, 'primitive' human existence, whether in the form of the noble savage, the peasant or the outcast from society; children who are uncorrupted by society's rigid way of comprehending the world; ghost stories, legends, myths and dreams. (iii) The self. As wisdom and morality are conceived in terms of an individual's response to the world outside rather than as a coherent collection of reasoned ideas and opinions, the writers turn in on themselves and try to explain and evaluate their living relationship with the world about them. (iv) Corresponding with the investigation of the self is a new detailed interest in nature, not for its own sake necessarily, but as a way of coming to understand the self. By understanding the individual's perception of the world of things outside, many 'nature poems' by Romantic writers try to explore the complicated relationships between things, feelings and ideas. William Wordsworth (1770–1850) and Percy Bysshe Shelley (1792–1822) go so far as to attempt to connect the development of moral values with the act of looking at a landscape. (v) 'Imagination' is a key word for understanding Romanticism. For many poets of the Romantic period the imagination represents the mind's power to create harmonious meaning out of the chaos of impressions, ideas, feelings and memories that inhabit it at any one moment. It is a shaping and creative power: its visitation gives joy, and its waning and loss are a cause for lamentation. (vi) A typical aspect of Romanticism is a yearning aspiration towards something beyond the ordinary world, not necessarily religious, which gives rise to symbolism, both as a way of looking at the world and as a poetic or literary technique. (vii) A departure from the 'rules of poetry' which dominated the earlier literary period (from 1660 to about 1800, referred to as the 'Neoclassical period'); spontaneity, creativity and the need to allow poems to shape themselves 'organically' (rather than according to rules or reason) are all valued ideals. (viii) Rebellion not only against poetic stultification, but against outmoded political institutions.

The apparent idealism of the French Revolution (1789) inspired many of the writers of the Romantic period. Many of the values and interests of this period remained alive right through the nineteenth century and are absorbed into modern literature

satire is the scornful ridiculing of topical issues, vice or folly; humour and irony are used to attack the objects of satire rather than to evoke mirth or pleasure

stream of consciousness a common narrative technique in the modern novel: the attempt to convey all the contents of a character's mind – memory, sense perceptions, feelings, intuitions, thoughts – in relation to the stream of experience as it passes by, often at random

structuralism dismisses the idea that language is 'natural' and can be used unproblematically as a mirror to reality. Structuralists see language not as a neutral means of communication, but as a self-enclosed system and as a code.

A basic tenet of structuralism is that meaning is not inherent in words, but depends on their mutual relationships within the system of language, a system based on difference. Structuralism argues that a text is a system in which language does not refer to 'reality' but only to itself and the patterns created within the text. Literature as a whole is also perceived as a self-referential system or structure and literary texts refer to each other. 'Intertextuality' is a term used to describe the many and various kinds of relationship that exist between texts, such as adaptation, translation, imitation, allusion, plagiarism and parody

trope a word or phrase used figuratively in a way that alters the usual or literal meaning; common tropes include metaphor, simile, metonymy, synecdoche and personification

AUTHOR OF THIS NOTE

Kathryn Simpson is Visiting Lecturer in English at Wolverhampton University, Birmingham University School of Continuing Studies, and Wulfrun College of Further Education in Wolverhampton. She received her B.A. and Ph.D. in English from Birmingham University.

York Notes Advanced (£3.99 each)

Margaret Atwood
The Handmaid's Tale

Jane Austen
Mansfield Park

Jane Austen
Persuasion

Jane Austen
Pride and Prejudice

Alan Bennett
Talking Heads

William Blake
Songs of Innocence and of Experience

Charlotte Brontë
Jane Eyre

Emily Brontë
Wuthering Heights

Geoffrey Chaucer
The Franklin's Tale

Geoffrey Chaucer
General Prologue to the Canterbury Tales

Geoffrey Chaucer
The Wife of Bath's Prologue and Tale

Joseph Conrad
Heart of Darkness

Charles Dickens
Great Expectations

John Donne
Selected Poems

George Eliot
The Mill on the Floss

F. Scott Fitzgerald
The Great Gatsby

E.M. Forster
A Passage to India

Brian Friel
Translations

Thomas Hardy
The Mayor of Casterbridge

Thomas Hardy
Tess of the d'Urbervilles

Seamus Heaney
Selected Poems from Opened Ground

Nathaniel Hawthorne
The Scarlet Letter

James Joyce
Dubliners

John Keats
Selected Poems

Christopher Marlowe
Doctor Faustus

Arthur Miller
Death of a Salesman

Toni Morrison
Beloved

William Shakespeare
Antony and Cleopatra

William Shakespeare
As You Like It

William Shakespeare
Hamlet

William Shakespeare
King Lear

William Shakespeare
Measure for Measure

William Shakespeare
The Merchant of Venice

William Shakespeare
Much Ado About Nothing

William Shakespeare
Othello

William Shakespeare
Romeo and Juliet

William Shakespeare
The Tempest

William Shakespeare
The Winter's Tale

Mary Shelley
Frankenstein

Alice Walker
The Color Purple

Oscar Wilde
The Importance of Being Earnest

Tennessee Williams
A Streetcar Named Desire

John Webster
The Duchess of Malfi

W.B. Yeats
Selected Poems

GCSE and equivalent levels (£3.50 each)

Maya Angelou
I Know Why the Caged Bird Sings

Jane Austen
Pride and Prejudice

Alan Ayckbourn
Absent Friends

Elizabeth Barrett Browning
Selected Poems

Robert Bolt
A Man for All Seasons

Harold Brighouse
Hobson's Choice

Charlotte Brontë
Jane Eyre

Emily Brontë
Wuthering Heights

Shelagh Delaney
A Taste of Honey

Charles Dickens
David Copperfield

Charles Dickens
Great Expectations

Charles Dickens
Hard Times

Charles Dickens
Oliver Twist

Roddy Doyle
Paddy Clarke Ha Ha Ha

George Eliot
Silas Marner

George Eliot
The Mill on the Floss

William Golding
Lord of the Flies

Oliver Goldsmith
She Stoops To Conquer

Willis Hall
The Long and the Short and the Tall

Thomas Hardy
Far from the Madding Crowd

Thomas Hardy
The Mayor of Casterbridge

Thomas Hardy
Tess of the d'Urbervilles

Thomas Hardy
The Withered Arm and other Wessex Tales

L.P. Hartley
The Go-Between

Seamus Heaney
Selected Poems

Susan Hill
I'm the King of the Castle

Barry Hines
A Kestrel for a Knave

Louise Lawrence
Children of the Dust

Harper Lee
To Kill a Mockingbird

Laurie Lee
Cider with Rosie

Arthur Miller
The Crucible

Arthur Miller
A View from the Bridge

Robert O'Brien
Z for Zachariah

Frank O'Connor
My Oedipus Complex and other stories

George Orwell
Animal Farm

J.B. Priestley
An Inspector Calls

Willy Russell
Educating Rita

Willy Russell
Our Day Out

J.D. Salinger
The Catcher in the Rye

William Shakespeare
Henry IV Part 1

William Shakespeare
Henry V

William Shakespeare
Julius Caesar

William Shakespeare
Macbeth

William Shakespeare
The Merchant of Venice

William Shakespeare
A Midsummer Night's Dream

William Shakespeare
Much Ado About Nothing

William Shakespeare
Romeo and Juliet

William Shakespeare
The Tempest

William Shakespeare
Twelfth Night

George Bernard Shaw
Pygmalion

Mary Shelley
Frankenstein

R.C. Sherriff
Journey's End

Rukshana Smith
Salt on the snow

John Steinbeck
Of Mice and Men

Robert Louis Stevenson
Dr Jekyll and Mr Hyde

Jonathan Swift
Gulliver's Travels

Robert Swindells
Daz 4 Zoe

Mildred D. Taylor
Roll of Thunder, Hear My Cry

Mark Twain
Huckleberry Finn

James Watson
Talking in Whispers

William Wordsworth
Selected Poems

A Choice of Poets

Mystery Stories of the Nineteenth Century including The Signalman

Nineteenth Century Short Stories

Poetry of the First World War

Six Women Poets

Chinua Achebe
Things Fall Apart

Edward Albee
Who's Afraid of Virginia Woolf?

Margaret Atwood
Cat's Eye

Jane Austen
Emma

Jane Austen
Northanger Abbey

Jane Austen
Sense and Sensibility

Samuel Beckett
Waiting for Godot

Robert Browning
Selected Poems

Robert Burns
Selected Poems

Angela Carter
Nights at the Circus

Geoffrey Chaucer
The Merchant's Tale

Geoffrey Chaucer
The Miller's Tale

Geoffrey Chaucer
The Nun's Priest's Tale

Samuel Taylor Coleridge
Selected Poems

Daniel Defoe
Moll Flanders

Daniel Defoe
Robinson Crusoe

Charles Dickens
Bleak House

Charles Dickens
Hard Times

Emily Dickinson
Selected Poems

Carol Ann Duffy
Selected Poems

George Eliot
Middlemarch

T.S. Eliot
The Waste Land

T.S. Eliot
Selected Poems

Henry Fielding
Joseph Andrews

E.M. Forster
Howards End

John Fowles
The French Lieutenant's Woman

Robert Frost
Selected Poems

Elizabeth Gaskell
North and South

Stella Gibbons
Cold Comfort Farm

Graham Greene
Brighton Rock

Thomas Hardy
Jude the Obscure

Thomas Hardy
Selected Poems

Joseph Heller
Catch-22

Homer
The Iliad

Homer
The Odyssey

Gerard Manley Hopkins
Selected Poems

Aldous Huxley
Brave New World

Kazuo Ishiguro
The Remains of the Day

Ben Jonson
The Alchemist

Ben Jonson
Volpone

James Joyce
A Portrait of the Artist as a Young Man

Philip Larkin
Selected Poems

D.H. Lawrence
The Rainbow

D.H. Lawrence
Selected Stories

D.H. Lawrence
Sons and Lovers

D.H. Lawrence
Women in Love

John Milton
Paradise Lost Bks I & II

John Milton
Paradise Lost Bks IV & IX

Thomas More
Utopia

Sean O'Casey
Juno and the Paycock

George Orwell
Nineteen Eighty-four

John Osborne
Look Back in Anger

Wilfred Owen
Selected Poems

Sylvia Plath
Selected Poems

Alexander Pope
Rape of the Lock and other poems

Ruth Prawer Jhabvala
Heat and Dust

Jean Rhys
Wide Sargasso Sea

William Shakespeare
As You Like It

William Shakespeare
Coriolanus

William Shakespeare
Henry IV Pt 1

William Shakespeare
Henry V

William Shakespeare
Julius Caesar

William Shakespeare
Macbeth

William Shakespeare
Measure for Measure

William Shakespeare
A Midsummer Night's Dream

William Shakespeare
Richard II

William Shakespeare
Richard III

William Shakespeare
Sonnets

William Shakespeare
The Taming of the Shrew

William Shakespeare
Twelfth Night

William Shakespeare
The Winter's Tale

George Bernard Shaw
Arms and the Man

George Bernard Shaw
Saint Joan

Muriel Spark
The Prime of Miss Jean Brodie

John Steinbeck
The Grapes of Wrath

John Steinbeck
The Pearl

Tom Stoppard
Arcadia

Tom Stoppard
*Rosencrantz and Guildenstern
are Dead*

Jonathan Swift
*Gulliver's Travels and The
Modest Proposal*

Alfred, Lord Tennyson
Selected Poems

W.M. Thackeray
Vanity Fair

Virgil
The Aeneid

Edith Wharton
The Age of Innocence

Tennessee Williams
Cat on a Hot Tin Roof

Tennessee Williams
The Glass Menagerie

Virginia Woolf
Mrs Dalloway

Virginia Woolf
To the Lighthouse

William Wordsworth
Selected Poems

Metaphysical Poets